DIEGO'S STORY

DIEGO'S STORY

*An extraordinary portrait of
willpower, love and life across two worlds*

Diego Soto

As told to Jill Rutherford

All publisher's proceeds will be donated to
THE JENNIFER TRUST FOR
SPINAL MUSCULAR ATROPHY

VERMILION
London

1 3 5 7 9 10 8 6 4 2

First published by Vermilion
an imprint of Ebury Press, Random House,
20 Vauxhall Bridge Rd,
London, SW1V 2SA

Random House Australia (Pty) Limited
20 Alfred Street, Milsons Point, Sydney,
New South Wales 2061, Australia

Random House New Zealand Limited
18 Poland Road, Glenfield
Auckland 10, New Zealand

Random House South Africa (Pty) Limited
PO Box 2263, Rosebank 2121, South Africa

Random House UK Limited Reg. No. 954009

Printed and bound in Great Britain by Mackays of Chatham plc, Kent

A CIP catalogue record for this book is available from the British Library

ISBN : 0 09 178554 5

While all the events described in this autobiography are true,
the names of some of the people have been altered.

For
My Mother, her family and my brother

In memory of
Orlando Snr (Eduardo in the book)
Great Grandmother Felisa
Great Aunts Chela, Hilda and Esneda
Sylvia Garner

My grateful thanks to
Jill, for obvious reasons
Dorothy Russel, for hours of typing
Colin, for his unfailing practical help
and friendship
Nick, for widening my horizons through his
knowledge and wisdom
My Mother, for her devotion, love and sacrifce
and for her optimistic and joyful nature
My brother, for always being prepared to stand in
for Mum and for putting up with me

Contents

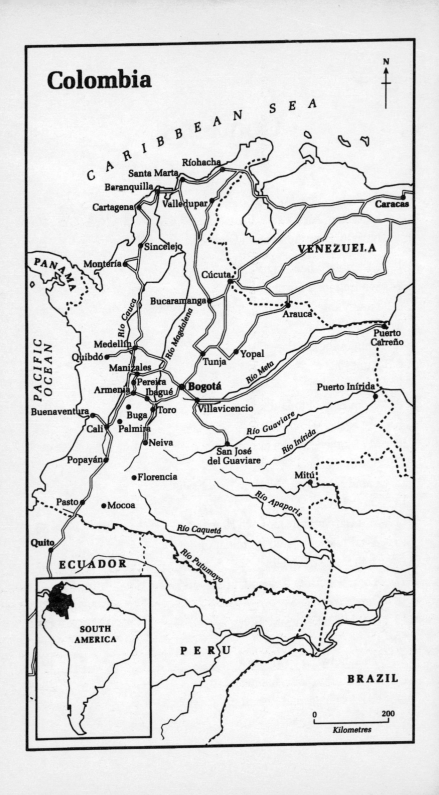

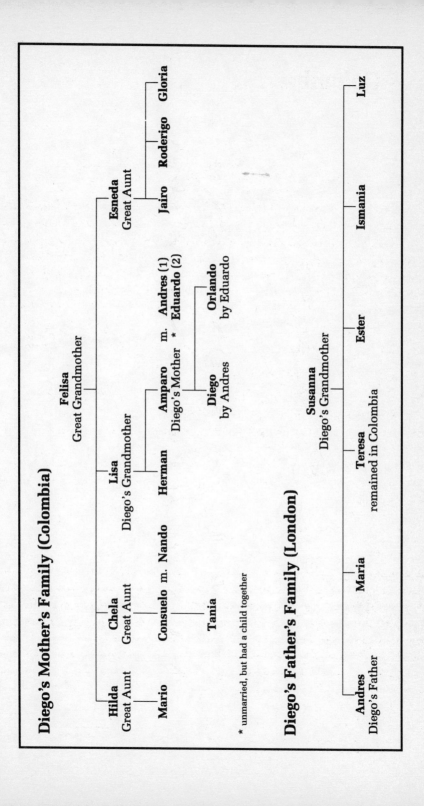

Diego's Mother's Family (Colombia)

Felisa
Great Grandmother

Hilda
Great Aunt

Chela
Great Aunt

Lisa
Diego's Grandmother

Esneda
Great Aunt

Mario

Consuelo m. **Nando**

Herman

Amparo m. **Andres (1)**
Diego's Mother * **Eduardo (2)**

Jairo **Roderigo** **Gloria**

Tania

Diego
by Andres

Orlando
by Eduardo

* unmarried, but had a child together

Diego's Father's Family (London)

Susanna
Diego's Grandmother

Andres
Diego's Father

Maria

Teresa
remained in Colombia

Ester

Ismania

Luz

ACKNOWLEDGMENTS

The publishers would like to thank the following for their
generous contribution to this book:

Bob Vickers for design; Robin Anderson and Sarah Reddington at
Slatter Anderson for cover design; Keren Levy for editorial work;
Creative Design and Print, London, for cover origination and
printing; Mackays of Chatham plc for printing and binding;
Paper Management Services, Kings Langley, Hertfordshire, for
supplying paper; David Perrott of Perrott Cartographics,
Machynlleth for map design and Business Colour Print, Welshpool
for outputting; Anita Macaulay of The Jennifer Trust for Spinal
Muscular Atrophy.

IN RECOGNITION OF THE WORK DONE AND HELP
GIVEN BY THE NATIONAL HEALTH SERVICE

An Extraordinary Life

by Jill Rutherford

Diego Soto was born in Columbia 21 years ago. He spends his life lying on his side or sitting in a wheelchair with the aid of a head support and body brace. He is unable to move any part of his body except for three fingers on the left hand. These he uses to activate the intercom and telephone system which provide his only means of independence. His mother and seventeen year old brother attend to such daily needs as dressing, toileting, washing and feeding as well as to his frequent requests to for his head or limbs to be moved when their position causes discomfort.

Diego suffers from Spinal Muscular Atrophy, a genetically inherited condition of the nerve cells in the spinal cord which results in progressive weakening and wasting of the muscles. It also affects the respiratory system, causing difficulties in breathing and coughing. Even minor chest infections may have serious consequences.

Spinal muscular Atrophy takes various forms, the most severe of which results in death before the age of two. Children with the mildest form often manage to sit, crawl and walk, albeit slowly. They can normally look forward to a long and active life.

Diego displayed symptoms of the condition in early infancy. As a small child he had a certain amount of strength in his back and neck, but could not sit unsupported. Although they were always weak, he was able to use his arms and fingers quite effectively for several years. As the condition progressed Diego maintained some form of independence with the aid of a computer and an electric wheelchair. But by the age of fifteen he no longer had the strength to use either effectively. Diego has never walked. Lack of use has given him small undeveloped stiff-jointed limbs. His legs are now permanently contracted to an angle of 90° and his chest is somewhat misshapen due to the effort of breathing with inadequate muscles. However, over the years, he has perfected the art of abdominal breathing.

I first met Diego in the Summer Term of 1991. As a hospital teacher I would start the day by visiting the paediatric wards to register the school-aged patients. As I peered into his cubicle I noticed that the bed slopped backwards towards the head signifying that the occupant must be suffering from a severe chest infection. A small, somewhat misshapen figure lay motionless. Plastic tubes sprouted from the veins in both arms. A large head was crowned with a shock of thick black hair and the face was obscured by an oxygen mask. I am ashamed to remember my first thoughts at the sight in front of me. Clearly I would not be able to contribute much to the education of this unfortunate child who may well have difficulty in communicating intelligibly. Nevertheless I ought to go through the motions.

Once I was sitting by the bed I could look more closely at my new pupil. I was immediately struck by a pair of large intelligent brown eyes and an engaging smile as Diego struggled to speak through the mask.

On discovering that I was a teacher he launched into the history of his disjointed and unsatisfactory education. He spoke articulately of an urgent need to prove himself and of his frustration at being in such a position through circumstance, certainly not through lack of ability.

As I listened, I found myself astonished and impressed at the confidence, self-belief and even a kind of arrogance manifested by this youth whose sixteen years had been overshadowed by the progress of a condition which was both crippling and life-threatening. There was no sign of self-pity or resentment; just pragmatic acceptance and a sense of impatience at the obstacles which prevented him from reaching his considerable potential.

Diego's hunger for adult conversation and debate dictated the format of our lessons. What started out as a discussion of literature soon turned into a vivid discourse on his own experiences, desire for knowledge and the awkward, and seemingly impossible, demands of puberty.

*

For Diego, these are doubly cruel, driven as he is by a deep need to discharge his duty as an adult Colombian male. However, I soon realised that, whatever the pressures it may bring, it is his greatly-cherished Colombian identity which gives Diego much of his strength and determination.

Paradoxically it is Diego's very difficulty in joining the brotherhood of macho men which has been an important influence on the shaping of a powerful personality. Forced to rely on inner resources, he has almost come close to turning his disability into an advantage.

A happy early childhood, spent in the company of loving relations, combined with innate self-belief and intelligence have given Diego the confidence to use any means at his disposal in order to achieve his goals. He has, per force, skilfully extracted whatever he needs from either situations or people. This he achieves with such courtesy, charm and self-deprecating humour that he is rarely denied.

For five years I have been a willing member of Diego's entourage. He and I have spent many entertaining hours discussing, arguing and laughing. His uncomplaining and optimistic attitude, as well as his enormous enjoyment of life, have been a lesson to me. I see him as he sees himself: a young man, looking forward enthusiastically to an exciting and challenging future, who just happens to be disabled.

Against All Odds

I am a cripple – or so I called myself (with relish) in my early teens. I did it to pre-empt the thoughts of people who stared at me, partly to shock and partly to break the ice. I used to enjoy their reactions, and gain confidence through their surprise that, in spite of my appearance, I was articulate and even intelligent.

When I was a little boy, I was well trained by my Great Aunt Chela's approach. If people stared at me, clearly thinking that I was much too old to still be in a pram, she would confront them at once. 'What are you looking at? Has he got a frog's head or something?' How easily it is assumed that a disabled body means a disabled mind.

With maturity my hostility towards such ignorance has lessened. Now I feel the need to educate people in their attitudes towards the disabled. I still feel angry about inequality, especially for the many who are worse off than me. Those who have perfectly good brains but not my cheek and demanding nature, rarely have a chance to prove themselves.

Surely people who are disabled have a right to fulfil their individual potential. I have had the good fortune to be given that chance. After many setbacks and false starts, I am on the way to achieving some of my goals. Opportunity arrived through a mixture of luck and persistence.

The doors to my future have opened, and all that can stop me walking through them is death. The muscular atrophy, which has gradually immobilised me and severely weakened my chest, keeps its shadow just around the corner, but I choose to ignore it. To me, it is more positive to live in what some might call 'cloud cuckoo-land', and to tell myself I am on an equal footing with the rest of society. At least for the moment. Who knows what may happen tomorrow. I could 'walk' under a bus. Not that I have any intention of doing so – there's far too much to accomplish. My body may not be up to much, but there's not too much wrong with my mind.

I feel that the sky's the limit, and I fully intend to confound all those who have told me to accept my lot or who assume that, being totally immobile, I must exist in a vegetative state.

I have already proved many people wrong by realising *some* of my dreams. Now I am working on the others.

Diego Soto
London 1997

1

The Early Years

One of the most important influences in my life has been my large and very close-knit family. I grew up surrounded by a host of doting aunts, uncles and cousins, all of whom believed that my disability made me special. I was given a sort of VIP status, and I have to admit that I loved it, even though it caused problems later when I started mixing with people who didn't share my family's views of me.

I was born in 1975 in Palmira, a city in south-west Colombia, when my mother, Amparo, was sixteen. She had been a schoolgirl, only fourteen years old, when she met my father, Andres, during one of her regular visits to her Aunt Esneda and her husband, in their small, two-storey house in Palmira. Mum was sent on an errand to a local shop, which involved passing a typical group of youths hanging about on a street corner who were 'sizing up the talent'. Andres was one of them. Before long, Mum had her first boyfriend. He was sixteen and lived with his mother, his five younger sisters and his grandmother. His father had left home after an argument and was not heard from again for twenty years.

Mum was completely smitten and returned home to the village of Toro to go back to school but determined to find a way of being near Andres. By the end of the school year, she had managed to persuade her mother, Lisa, to let her finish her education in Palmira, and she went to live with her Aunt Esneda. Once there, she lost no time in hatching a plot with Andres to get herself enrolled in his school.

Not long after her sixteenth birthday, Mum discovered that she was pregnant. Horrified and frightened, she fully expected to be beaten by her mother or her aunt. She tried to hide her condition from them but they sensed the truth and eventually forced her to confess. While they were still recovering from their shock and anger, Mum's Aunt Chela arrived from Toro, having heard the terrible news. Aunt Chela was the eldest of the sisters and a great organiser. She believed in 'doing the right thing', especially where religion was concerned, and was determined to defend the family honour by making sure that the young Andres carried out his responsibilities.

A deputation consisting of Aunt Chela, my grandmother and my mother went to speak to my grandfather to ask him to take responsibility for the situation. He was working as a tailor in Cali and had not been on the scene for many years. It was a pointless trip. He washed his hands of the whole situation, so instead the women visited Andres and his mother, Susanna, in an attempt to convince *them* that marriage was the only answer. But Andres' mother appeared to take the same attitude as grandfather. It seemed hopeless.

Luckily, the situation *was* eventually resolved (albeit briefly). Andres was banned from seeing my mother which, human nature being what it is, of course drove him straight into her arms. In an act of teenage rebellion, they met in secret and agreed to get married immediately, courtesy of a rather irregular priest who was known to marry under-age couples without bothering about any tedious legalities or parental permission.

After the ceremony, where a couple of friends attended as witnesses, my parents went back to their respective households. Mum packed her belongings and then went to bed as usual. The first that the rest of the household knew of her change of status was when Andres arrived the next day to collect his wife and take her home. His own mother, presented with her brand-new daughter-in-law, was then honour-bound to welcome her into the already over-crowded house.

There was a terrible fuss. Both my parents had to leave school, with no qualifications. Andres found a job operating a machine which pumped toothpaste into tubes. But worse was to come. Within weeks of her wedding, Mum realised that she and Andres had nothing in common. She was attractive, vivacious and gregarious, and he was quiet, introverted and obviously finding his new responsibilities a tremendous strain. At first, my mother tried to be a proper Colombian wife, cleaning, cooking and washing for her husband, but after a very short time she knew that a lifetime with this unresponsive stranger was impossible to contemplate. There was only one thing she could do. She went back home, still pregnant.

Coincidentally, my mother's aunt, Esneda was also pregnant at this time. Almost six months later, in October, both women gave birth during the same week. Aunt Esneda's baby was my second cousin Gloria.

By now, most of our family disapproved so strongly of Andres that they refused to let him see his new son. However, Aunt Esneda felt differently, believing that Andres had a right to see me. She would take me out in my pram and make sure that we bumped into my father every now and then. Apparently, this kind-hearted scheme was eventually abandoned when Aunt Esneda realised that the young Andres was quite indifferent as to whether he saw me or not.

[Not long after this time, Andres' mother, Susanna, left Columbia to live in England. He eventually followed her. Andres worked as a waiter at the Sheraton Hotel in Kensington, and Mum did not hear from him again. About four years later, he went to a Latin American night club in London where a fire broke out. The fire doors were locked, causing complete panic, and many young people died, including my father who was only twenty-three.]

Now that my mother's embarrassing bump had turned into me, my grandmother decided that there was nothing to stop her going back to school and finishing her education. People had short memories, she said, they would soon forget about the disgrace that had been brought on the family. So, while continuing to work in Cali (which meant getting up at 5 o' clock every morning), my grandmother rented a room in Palmira. We all moved in and my mother went back to school.

Secondary schools in Colombia fall into two categories – those which are purely academic and those which are more orientated towards vocational studies. Places in these schools were scarce enough twenty years ago, when Mum resumed her education, but *now* things are so bad that each school building in the large towns is used by three different schools each day. The first school starts at 7 am, the second at 1 pm and the third at 6 pm.

While Mum was at school, Aunt Esneda looked after her own

baby, Gloria, and me. Her sons, Roderigo and Jairo were at primary school. Her husband, Simon, had a menial job working for the town council as a truck driver. There was little money coming into the family and the situation was complicated by the fact that their home consisted of only the ground floor. They planned to extend it, as is the Colombian custom, when their finances allowed. But, eighteen years later, it is still not complete.

My grandmother and mother were also struggling. By the end of each month there was often no money left, not even for baby milk. Sometimes things became so bad that Felisa, my great-grandmother, would be driven to stealing powdered milk from her daughter, Aunt Esneda, to give to her granddaughter, my mother! Eventually, money became so tight that my mother had to look for a part-time job, even though she was still at school. With the help of a friend, she got some clerical work in a furniture factory. This same friend changed our lives – she introduced Mum to Eduardo.

Eduardo would come to see Mum every night after dinner. Mind you, it wasn't exactly a comfortable arrangement. They had to stand on the doorstep each night, as is the Colombian custom, to make sure their courtship took place in the public eye, while allowing them to get away from the more piercing gaze of the family. Suitors were only invited in on special occasions.

Before long they were in love and the relationship quickly became serious. Aunt Chela, mindful as ever of what she considered to be her duty, decided to test the young man. One evening, during the ritual courtship routine, she ordered her ten-year-old nephew to appear on the doorstep, carrying me. He did as he was told, handing the screaming bundle to my mother. The results were not what Aunt Chela had anticipated. Although clearly surprised by my sudden entrance, Eduardo accepted the situation quite calmly. Mum had already told him about me.

Within a few weeks, Mum, Eduardo and I were living together as a family in a rented room. Although this meant living in uncomfortable and cramped conditions, the young couple hardly noticed the inconvenience because, in Latin American countries, so much time is spent out in the open. In Britain, family life revolves around the living room and the television. In Colombia, it takes place on the doorstep.

Although they were not married, Eduardo took his new responsibilities very seriously. He left school. At first, this was a disaster. He had been at an academic school so it had been assumed he would go on to further education, but now he was not qualified for anything. For about a year, we scraped by on the money Eduardo earned from recycling car parts which he rescued from junk yards and polished up for sale. Eduardo insisted that Mum should stop working which enabled her to complete her education, but it was a hard time for them.

What saved us all in the end was a small inheritance left by Eduardo's father. There wasn't much of it, as most of his money had gone on the huge medical bills incurred during his long illness, but he did leave a large empty factory which had once been used for the family business. Having worked in a furniture factory, Mum knew how much profit could be made from the painting and firing stages of furniture manufacture. As there were very few kilns around at the time, Mum suggested that Eduardo should install one. Her instinct changed our lives. Eduardo invited his brothers to join him in this venture, but they laughed and refused to part with a penny. Fortunately, his mother and an uncle were able to lend him enough to be able to start his business.

As soon as the business started to make money and Eduardo was able to manufacture his own furniture, his family swarmed around him like bees round a honeypot! Eventually, he decided to make everything over to his mother, preferring to start up again on his own. By now he was able to rent a small house and he bought himself his first motor bike. Over the following years he was to go bankrupt several times, but somehow he always managed to pick himself up and start again.

During the time Eduardo was running the factory, he and my mother worked around the clock, often having barely enough to eat. Yet Eduardo made sure that I never went without. What's more, he treated me like a son, and I called him Dad. Until I was about four, I really believed that Eduardo was my father. He could not have been a better one, devoting hours of his spare time to me. In spite of his own youth, he was mature in many ways and had his own methods of winning respect as well as love. Unlike many

Colombian fathers, he never got the belt out. Nothing was too much trouble or too expensive.

I shall never forget my delight when he presented me, at the age of 7, with a beautifully-made pair of fancy cowboy boots. The fact that I would never be able to walk in them made no difference to my pride whenever I wore them. I adored them. Some of the most special times for me were when I had Eduardo all to myself on our motor bike outings. During our lives together, he took care of me and did all the paternal things that any father would do. He was just the way I'd like to be if I ever have any children.

When Mum was twenty-one she became pregnant again and things changed. It was obvious to her that the new baby would always come first with Eduardo, because it would be his own child. It wasn't obvious to me because at this time I thought he was my real father. Although I was only four, Mum regarded me as much more intelligent than other children of my own age. She decided to tell me the truth. I remember her lying down on the bed beside me one day at siesta time and saying: 'Eduardo is not your father.' I thought she was joking, and almost laughed. I didn't believe it at first, but she was adamant. It felt like a game. My first reaction was to think 'How exciting to have two dads'! That evening, when Eduardo walked into the house, I shouted: 'You're not my dad! My dad is someone else.' Eduardo was stunned. He and Mum had a terrible argument, then he turned to me and said something which I didn't understand at first, but now realise was along the lines of 'You ungrateful little sod'. Perhaps he felt I was rejecting him.

I can see now that things were never again quite the same between us. Although he still provided for me materially, the emotional bond had been weakened. I never called him Dad again, and he no longer referred to me as his son and we rarely did things on our own together. But he was still my hero, and the man I most wanted to be.

He was certainly no saint however. Even during Mum's pregnancy, Eduardo was unfaithful to her. As soon as he could afford it, he chose to conform to the pattern of behaviour established by almost all Colombian men. It is not uncommon for each husband to have a series of mistresses, discarding them without a second's thought when he is tired of them. Most of the wives turn a blind eye to such infidelities as long as they are provided for. After all, a new mistress for their husband *could* mean the latest fridge-freezer for the kitchen! However, they also know that if *they* are unfaithful, or cause too many scenes about their rivals, they will be abandoned. Traditional Colombian masculine behaviour is full of double standards.

I first became aware that Eduardo was straying well before Mum's pregnancy, while he was building up his first business. As soon as there was some spare cash, he would disappear for whole weekends. Each Friday afternoon, the workers were paid and Mum was given her housekeeping money. Eduardo would then tell her that he had to put the car in the garage down the road, and that was the last we would see of him until Sunday night. He was the dutiful husband and father during the week, but during the weekends he would let himself off the leash and practise his considerable charm and 'gift of the gab' on a succession of beautiful girls.

Mum hated it, of course. She was young, attractive and full of life, but that wasn't enough for Eduardo. I remember there were lots of arguments and shouting matches, but they didn't alter anything. Every now and then Mum would march off to start a new course at evening class, to gain more qualifications so she could leave Eduardo and support us. It was a threat that she did not carry out until six years later.

I was 3$^{1}/_{2}$ when my brother, Orlando was born. That day, Eduardo was getting ready for one of his 'hunting' expeditions. His plans were ruined when Mum announced that the baby was coming. They carried me to the truck and took me to Aunt Esneda's on their way to the hospital. The next morning I was told that I had a brother. My longed for companion had arrived. Thank goodness it was a boy. We could have such fun together and I should no longer need to rely on soppy girls to play with and bend to my will. How proud I was that I should always be the elder brother whose duty it would be to protect and teach. Even at that tender age I was aware that my brother would be a most useful 'slave'. Indeed, by the time he was 18 months old, Orlando had somehow sensed that I had special needs. As he grew older he never questioned what Mum and I saw as his duty to help me in every possible way. It is only now, at seventeen, that he occasionally questions my constant demands.

One evening, not long after Orlando was born, Mum was at evening class and Eduardo was out. Orlando and I were being looked after by our great-grandmother, Felisa. Eduardo came home unexpectedly to check up on us on us and found a screaming baby, a helpless old woman and me. I, of course, could do nothing to help.

Eduardo took one look, scooped up Orlando and myself and carried us out to his flashy pick-up truck. I was ecstatic at the thought of going out with my hero again. Before long, we stopped and Eduardo collected a good-looking blonde. I remember thinking that it seemed rather fishy, but I dared not say a word. When she got into the truck, the girl noticed that I was quite unable to support myself on the slippery seat. She offered to sit me on her lap. I refused vehemently. To accept would have felt as if I were betraying Mum, which I had no intention if doing. However, an invitation like that today would be much harder to refuse!

Eduardo had told me not to breathe a word and I agreed. But, like a fool, as soon as I set eyes on Mum I couldn't stop myself shouting: 'I know something you don't!' Eventually, Mum wormed it out of me. Eduardo could hardly chastise me because that would mean admitting his own deception and losing my respect. But it was the last time he took me out without Mum for many years.

Although I felt sad for Mum, watching her humiliation over Eduardo's girlfriends, I never really blamed him. It didn't occur to me, as a little boy, that he owed her anything. Once I knew that I was not his son, I felt it was wrong to expect too much from him. Perhaps it got under his skin that Mum was still married to Andres and could not marry him. Whatever the truth of the matter, I still admired and hero-worshipped the man, fantasising that I would grow up to be exactly like him.

It was thanks to Eduardo that I gained the confidence and belief in myself that have carried me through my life. As well as giving me the security I felt in our little family, Eduardo was responsible for saving my life several times. I shall always be grateful to him for that.

2

Waiting for A Miracle

I weighed 9¹/₂ pounds at birth. Large babies are considered beautiful in Colombia – but I wasn't the healthy child that I appeared to be. By the time I was six months old the wound where my umbilical cord had been cut still hadn't healed, so my mother took me to a doctor. He prescribed a series of injections in my stomach. Soon afterwards I became very ill with what seemed to be flu, causing vomiting, coughing and difficulty in breathing. Eventually I got better, but began to lose weight, and my cousins of the same age, once much smaller, overtook me in size.

It was obvious that I wasn't developing properly. I could not lift my head or sit up without support, but to begin with, no-one worried too much. My great-grandmother always told Mum that she had given birth to twelve children and two of them had been late developers. It was nothing to be concerned about. Mum accepted this reasoning and waited, trusting in her elders and in God.

Over many months I continued to get chest infections and high temperatures. On one occasion I had such serious convulsions that the doctor sent me home to die. Somehow I hung on and survived. On another occasion, when I was about two, my lungs filled with fluid. I could hardly breathe and began to turn blue. Eduardo rushed me to hospital, carried me into the reception area and demanded to see a doctor. All the receptionist was interested in was whether he had a bank account and, if so, what was the number? He left her talking to herself and rushed me upstairs to the doctors. I was saved!

Eduardo was always cool-headed whenever I was sick, which was just as well because Mum would panic and become quite hysterical if I was really ill. Sometimes she would totally break down, lock herself in the wardrobe and refuse to come out. She relied on Eduardo completely. When it came to me, he never let her down and, whenever my health was in jeopardy, made sure I saw the best doctors that he could afford.

As I grew older, it became impossible to ignore my condition. My body was very floppy and my limbs were small and under-developed. Desperate to find a cause, and therefore a cure, we visit-ed doctor after doctor. They all agreed that something was seriously wrong, but each one had a different theory as to what it was. I was very thin; perhaps it was due to the sweats I suffered from, or to malnutrition (this was a great insult to Mum). Or maybe it was cerebral palsy, although not all the symptoms fitted. I was six years old when my illness was finally diagnosed.

We had gone to see a distinguished orthopaedic surgeon at the Cali University Hospital. He took a biopsy of some muscle tissue and told Mum that I had been born with muscular atrophy – a disease similar to muscular dystrophy, in which your muscles deteriorate until you are completely incapacitated. It didn't mean much to her; I suppose it sounded like just another theory. Anyway, Mum didn't set much store by doctors – she was waiting for God to cure me. She was sure that, when He felt the time was right, He would make me walk. It was just a matter of waiting patiently for the miracle to happen.

At times, my illness caused me considerable pain. I may not have had much movement in my body, but I could certainly feel everything. Once the doctors had diagnosed muscular atrophy they prescribed a body brace – a rather primitive affair made from plastic and containing big metal bars and plates. When I put it on, it felt as though it didn't fit me – hardly surprising because it had been made too large on purpose, so that I could grow into it. As a result, it was extremely uncomfortable. I hated it but knew that I had to wear it. This was my treatment and it would cure me. Besides, it had cost Eduardo a fortune, and Mum and Aunt Esneda had taken me on long journeys to and from hospital for the fittings, consultations and medication. I couldn't let them all down by refus-ing to wear it, although even Mum did not really believe in it. We were all still waiting for the miracle.

I spent a lot of time in Eduardo's furniture factory, sitting on the desk in his office. It was a good vantage point for watching every-thing which happened on the factory floor. I would sit for hours gazing at the men working. At the age of five I had appointed myself a sort of foreman. In reality, I was more of a spy! I gaily reported any laziness or time-wasting to Eduardo, quite impervious to the fact that the staff all hated me, especially when I was presented with my wages like everyone else at the end of the week.

One day I was sitting on the desk as usual, wearing the instrument of torture. At this stage my limbs had not stiffened up completely, so I was able to balance with my legs apart. I looked down and noticed my baby brother crawling around on the floor. I was playing with a rubber band and Orlando wanted it. I knew he would have no trouble taking it from me, so I tried to hide it between my legs. As I bent forward to tuck the elastic band out of the way, the bottom of the brace dug into my thigh. My femur snapped.

The pain was so excruciating that I could do nothing but scream. Mum rushed in and removed the brace, but as I couldn't say a word and all she could see was a large lump, she rubbed my leg – the traditional Colombian remedy for a bruise. The pain continued for the rest of that day, all that night, and all through the following day. To add to the discomfort, well-meaning people rubbed alcohol into the 'bruise', causing yet more agony.

Eventually, Mum took me to the hospital, carrying me in the only way she knew (and which she still uses), which is with one arm supporting my back and the other under my knees. If you have a broken femur, this is hardly the most comfortable means of transport!

As soon as I was seen by the doctors they realised what was wrong. They fitted me up with a drip and within seconds I was unconscious. I woke up as happy as a lark, the pain gone. There was a plaster cast covering one leg and half-way down the other. Years later, I was told that the doctors had used far too much plaster. Perhaps they were taking the opportunity to charge as much as possible because the bill was certainly huge.

I wore the cast for six weeks. At last it was time to take the plaster off. I am not sure if bad circulation is the cause, but I have always had very tender joints, especially in my toes, ankles and knees; whenever they are knocked, it feels as if they have been dislocated. I was prepared for the extra pain of having to bend my legs after having them kept absolutely straight for six weeks, but I certainly was not ready for what happened during the removal of my cast. The doctor picked up his pair of huge scissors, opened them wide and thrust them through it, smashing them on to my knee in the process. That was the start of three more weeks of agonising pain. I still remember the horror of having my underpants put on and taken off every day. Each time I was lifted up, my leg flopped down at the knee, whilst I nearly went through the roof! I was not in pain if I kept absolutely still, but Mum insisted on clean bedclothes daily. I dreaded the agonising moves from bed to bed for the sheet-changing ritual.

3

Family Life

Although I was often ill and could not move around like other children, it was something I mostly accepted without question. I was loved and cared for – spoilt, actually – by my extended family. No one minded carrying me, pushing me in a pram, or seeing to all my needs. In fact, I was often made to feel special, perhaps partly because I was unusually articulate from an early age. I felt smarter and more mature than my contemporaries, although at times I resorted to childish tantrums when I could not get my own way. I remember the frustration of feeling that I had been tied down, unable to move no matter how much I wanted to.

I soon learned to turn situations to my advantage. I had an imaginary friend and, if something went wrong or I had been naughty, it was always his fault. If I was being greedy, it was always he who had asked for more food. Not that I lacked company – my many aunts and cousins made sure I was never lonely. My mother's three aunts played an especially important part in my childhood. As well as Aunt Esneda in Palmira, I was often sent to stay with Aunt Chela in Toro, and Aunt Hilda, who lived nearby. I loved these visits, which began in the early days when Mum and Eduardo went on a sort of honeymoon.

Believing she knew what was best for everyone, Aunt Chela was very kind and protective, and wrapped me in cotton wool. I soon learned to manipulate her. Even Aunt Chela's grand-daughter, Tania, took second place while I was around although I don't think she ever resented it. Like most of my contemporaries, she saw me as a baby, whatever my age. I was always being carried or pushed, dressed and fed, so I was not a real threat. However, my power lay in speech. Both adults and children were amazed at my ability to talk to anyone. I revelled in using the power of language to my advantage. I memorised hundreds of what I thought were useful and clever phrases on a wide range of subjects, and I would produce a few of them, like rabbits out of a hat, whenever I got the chance. I realise now that I often had no idea what I was talking about, but that did not stop me airing my views at the first opportunity. Besides, the astonished expressions on the faces of my audience always spurred me on to even greater displays of brilliance!

Looking back, it was the reactions to these verbal tricks which helped to boost my confidence when I was very young – a feeling that's never left me. I've always known I can rely on my mind. My inert body, on the other hand, leaves a lot to be desired.

I became pretty good at swearing, too. Frustration sometimes made me curse everyone in sight, and I would rack my brains for every piece of invective I could think of. My mother thought this impertinent and always tried to shut me up, but both Aunt Chela and her mother, Felisa, would hotly defend my right to express my frustrations. After all, it was the only way open to me.

It was Aunt Chela who taught me how to read and write, to say my prayers and, above all, to recognise the importance of family loyalty. She was a great believer in tradition, and always maintained that there was one law for girls and another for boys, which there certainly is in Colombia.

My greatest fear was to be left alone, so each morning Aunt Chela would sit me in her rocking chair and put it in the wide corridor which connected all the rooms in the house. It meant I was able to see everything that was going on and talk to my aunt whilst she worked in the kitchen.

As far as Aunt Chela was concerned, I was not permanently disabled. She refused to accept the idea. Many were the times she would produce a strange-looking concoction, quite certain that rubbing it into my legs would bring about a cure. The poultice of boiled orange leaves was quite soothing and smelt lovely, but I wasn't so keen on the wax plasters. Plantain leaves, containing warmed and softened wax, were laid on my legs each night before I went to sleep. They would feel quite pleasant at first, but as the wax cooled it became more and more rigid. Then my legs would start to itch, driving me to distraction. Far from being able to sleep, I would lie in bed moaning and groaning, until Aunt Chela took pity on me and removed the offending plasters.

Despite the discomfort I suffered from some of her treatments, I always knew that Aunt Chela had my best interests at heart. She would have done anything within her power to help me walk, and I loved and trusted her, revelling in the attention she gave me. Even when I behaved badly, I could count on her being on my side, much to the disgust of my cousins. I suppose it was her way of trying to compensate for the cruel joke that Nature had played on me. As a result, I was allowed to get away with mischief which would never have been tolerated from the other children.

Aunt Chela was also responsible for laying the foundations of my Catholic faith. She observed all the religious festivals and taught me my prayers. Although I no longer practise my faith as I should, I still consider myself to be a devout Catholic and I am grateful to my great aunt for sowing the seeds of my religious conviction.

It is easy to re-live the joy I always felt when I was told that we were off to visit Chela's sister, Great Aunt Hilda who ran a boarding house. I would sit in my buggy, feeling thoroughly pleased with life, as we set off in the blazing sun, fanned by a welcoming breeze. The main road was lined with large, rather sprawling, traditionally built bungalows with flat, brown-tiled roofs and wooden verandas. The ceilings of their blue- or green-painted rooms were so high that it required a handyman on a ladder to change a light bulb, and residents were to be found sitting in the dark when no-one was available to help.

Sometimes we would see coffee beans laid out on pieces of sacking. They were being sun-roasted on the road in front of their owner's house. The few drivers to pass by always treated these obstacles with great respect. Although coffee is a valuable commodity in Colombia, there was never a problem with theft. If you put your coffee beans outside, you could be sure that they'd still be there when you came back for them.

At last we would arrive at Aunt Hilda's boarding house. There were three bedrooms, each containing four beds. My aunt's tenants were usually bus-drivers, council workers and policemen. But each August, at carnival time, the house was full of soldiers, members of brass bands or even bull-fighters!

Aunt Chela would push me through the house into the living

room, whilst I averted my eyes superstitiously, from the open door
leading into Aunt Hilda's bedroom, in case I should catch sight of
the bed in which her husband had died, or even worse, the picture
hanging above it. Here were depicted a mass of terrified sinners
burning in purgatory. I knew I would join them if I misbehaved.
But at least the picture offered a ray of hope – a few of these miserable souls were being pulled up through the clouds by heavenly
angels. I told myself that if I tried to be good, I might also be saved
and allowed to sit next to Jesus and Mary.

I was relieved to arrive in the cool corridor, where once again I
was placed so that I could sit looking into the kitchen, watching my
aunts cooking and cleaning for the boarders. Aunt Hilda always
had a treat waiting for me – fried slices of ripe plantain covered
with cream she had skimmed off the milk bought for her lodgers.
Bliss!

Aunt Chela and I made the most of our meals when we visited
Aunt Hilda, who could afford better chicken and more ice-cream
than others in the family. She also had running water in her
kitchen and had no need to collect it in buckets from the tank in the
corridor, as her sister did. In the afternoons, Aunt Chela would help
her sister to sell food. People would knock at the front door and
ask if any home-made ice-cream, soft drinks or beer were for sale.
Sometimes there would be a few eggs, if they had not been eaten
by the lodgers.

I looked forward to the arrival of Aunt Hilda's errand boys who
came three times a day to push a kind of wooden wheelbarrow
packed with food to the local prison. Aunt Hilda was employed by
the town council to provide all the inmates' meals. The boys
indulged me by playing the games I chose. My favourite entailed
being pushed in their wheelbarrow at break-neck speed, up and
down the corridor. At other times I ordered the construction of
elaborate cardboard and twig palaces in which I sat and held court.

Once all the work was over and the lodgers had gone to bed, my
aunts used to sit on the doorstep in the cool of the evening, chatting
to neighbours and passers-by. Then, at about 11 pm, Aunt Chela
and I would make our way back to her home through the deserted
streets. During these nocturnal journeys, Aunt Chela insisted on
carrying me instead of pushing me in the pram, which she would

leave behind for an errand boy to deliver the following morning. Worried about the effect of the night air on my weak chest, she would hold me close to the warmth of her own body and cover me in blankets. She must have looked as though she was struggling home clutching a bundle of laundry!

Superstition has always played a big part in the life of Colombia's country towns, and even highly-educated Colombians have a strong fear of the supernatural. I was brought up to believe that each road had its own ghostly inhabitant. The main road was the only one with any street lighting, and as we walked along it I would peep out in terror through my layers of blanket at the pitch-black side roads and alleyways, scanning the darkness for signs of spectral life. I never saw anything, but one of my great-uncles did. One night he spotted a beautiful woman dressed in green, weeping and apparently searching for something valuable. Having consumed substantial amounts of alcohol at one of the local brothels, he could hardly believe his luck. But as he went to comfort her, the object of his desire disappeared in front of his startled gaze. Instantly, he was sober!

Most children in Toro were brought up on a diet of ghost stories, the majority of which contained warnings about bad behaviour. Their elders would of course threaten them with ghostly visitations whenever they were naughty. Although convinced that my family's protection made me almost invincible, there was one spirit which held a mixture of terror and fascination for me. The *Duende* is the devil's son, the size of a child but with the face of an old man. His feet point backwards and he wears a black sombrero and a black cloak. This sinister gnome falls in love with innocent long-haired girls, materialising in their gardens at midnight and serenading them with his irresistible voice while playing a guitar. The only way a family can prevent this courtship is to hang a stringless guitar in the garden. When the *Duende* tries to play it, all that can be heard is the sound of his weeping.

Once we had negotiated our way through the ghost town, Aunt Chela and I would go to our bed. Because I cannot turn over without help, I have never slept on my own. Unable to exercise in any way, I often find it hard to get to sleep. After saying our prayers, my aunt and I would lie awake while she would tell me folk tales.

One evening, smarting from an injection of antibiotic I lay listening to the sounds of the night. By now, I could distinguish between many of the footsteps of the men returning home after a hard night's drinking and womanising. Suddenly, we were terrified to hear someone pushing hard at the front door. Was this the dreaded *Duende*? My aunt leaped out of bed, convinced that he was after her prized new acquisition, a 250cc Yamaha motorbike which she had won in a local raffle. Even though she had no idea how to ride it, this gleaming object held pride of place in the living room. It was worth a lot of money!

All Aunt Chela could do to prevent us being murdered in our beds was to try to barricade our bedroom door. As she struggled to close it, she knocked over a huge iron bar, kept there for protection like the two machetes lying under the bed. At the deafening sound of the metal hitting the tiled floor, the burglar fled. The *Duende* had been fooled again!

I received so much cosseting and tender loving care on my visits to my great-aunts in Toro that I was always reluctant to leave when Mum and Eduardo arrived to take me home. However, once we had left the countryside behind I would start to look forward to being in Palmira again.

4

Aunt Esneda

Eduardo often told me how much he missed me when I was away and I believed him at the time, but now I think his real motive for having me home again was that it meant Mum would be chained to the house while he went out gallivanting. Even so, I was always glad to be back in what I thought was the lap of luxury. We had a state-of-the-art record player, two colour televisions (status symbols – Colombian television is nothing to write home about!), a telephone, fashionable furniture and, best of all, the beautiful, shining, blue Chevrolet pick-up truck.

As Eduardo was usually out in the evenings, Mum, Orlando and I would spend them with Aunt Esneda, her daughter Gloria, who was my own age, and her sons Rodrigo and Jairo, who were a few years older. At about the time Mum set up home with Eduardo, her own mother left to find work in the cigar factories in Venezuela. She lived there alone for the next eleven years, during which time Aunt Esneda became Mum's greatest friend and confidante. Although her husband resented me, Esneda ignored his attitude and treated me as her own. It was she who took me on my daily visit to church each December. With Gloria in tow, she carried me to her local church for the children's Novena to Baby Jesus. I loved being in the house of God. I felt at home as I repeated the prayers, sometimes glancing up at one of the glittering statues in the hope that I should catch it in the act of blinking! As we made our way home I experienced a mixture of elation and contentment – God was in his heaven and all was right in the world.

Whenever I became ill, Aunt Esneda was the first person Mum turned to, in the knowledge that she could depend on the older woman's practical and moral support. I was always going for some medical test or other to the big teaching hospital in Cali, and when Mum took me we did things in style, travelling in luxury air-conditioned coaches or taxis. We had lunch in a smart restaurant at the bus terminal, and arrived home four hours after we had left. But Mum found these hospital visits upsetting and was grateful when Aunt Esneda offered to take me instead. Without this help, Mum could easily have become depressed about the length and frequency of my chest infections. In return, she did her aunt's housework and shopping.

Aunt Esneda would collect me at 8 o'clock in the morning, but instead of taking a taxi to the bus station, she carried me there. We would board an old bone-shaker of a bus which seemed to stop at every opportunity. The heat was intense, and the plastic seats burned my bottom, although my trendy Levis provided a little protection. All the passengers shouted at the tops of their voices, telling one another where to sit as the sweat poured down their faces. Babies were either screaming or being breast-fed; toddlers chased up and down the aisle. My aunt made sure she had hidden her pieces of jewellery and my precious gold ring in her purse. We clung to each other as we bounced along, but it was fun. I loved watching our noisy and colourful neighbours, whilst Aunt Esneda kept up a string of amusing remarks.

Eventually we arrived at the bus terminal in Cali, thoroughly battered by the journey. But again, there would be no taxi. Instead, we boarded a local bus, which was no mean feat. Queues rarely exist in Colombia. As the waiting crowd surged forward, I felt tense as I lay in Aunt Esneda's arms. We would be pushed from all directions by fellow travellers determined to grab seats. My greatest fear centred around the turnstiles just inside the entrance to the bus. One extra push would result in my dangling legs becoming tangled in the mechanism as my aunt was propelled forwards. Determined not to show my terror I would casually say 'Excuse me, aunt, please lift my legs up a little, if you don't mind.' Throughout my life I have become expert at anticipating pain and trying to find ways of minimising it.

On arrival at the hospital I faced the ordeal again as everyone tumbled out of the bus. Now came the tedious part of the day. Here there were queues - queues for everything and hours of waiting. After I had at last been seen by the doctor, it would be back to the bus pantomime. When we arrived at the terminal, there was no chance of the restaurant lunch I was used to with my mother.

Instead, Aunt Esneda would buy me a Supermalt drink, while persuading me that I had no desire whatsoever to eat 'in that horrible unhygienic restaurant'. I was unconvinced but there wasn't much I could do about it. Besides, I knew perfectly well what Aunt Esneda was doing – saving the money which Mum had provided for our meal, just as she had done with the travelling expenses. Even at the age of five or six I felt that I had no right to take away her chance to make a little 'pocket money' to spend on her own children.

The train cost even less than the bus, so now we made our way to the station. It seemed like many hours later when the train chugged in. I gazed in awe at the steam pouring from the funnel. How envious I felt of its power. It was a wild animal, temporarily tamed – truly an iron horse. We forced our way into a packed carriage to join our noisy fellow passengers, mostly peasants clutching sacks, boxes of chickens and babies. I envied the men's loose-fitting white cotton trousers and shirts, straw hats and brightly coloured leather bags. Their ponchos were folded across one shoulder, and their feet looked cool in rope sandals. But what thrilled me most was the sight of each man's machete in its elaborately decorated sheath, hanging from a heavy belt. I could picture him wielding his weapon in a fight for his honour or for that of the woman he loved. The women were equally colourful, in their long, swirling black skirts encircled with bands of bright satin. Their puff-sleeved white blouses were elasticated round the neck, and the younger women wore them pulled down over their shoulders – an exotic look which was enhanced by the large flower they pushed behind one ear. All the women wore their black hair in thick shining braids. They looked wonderful. Every now and then, there would be a shout above the general hubbub as a young man pushed his way through the crowd, selling confectionery from a wooden tray hanging round his neck.

When I grew bored with watching the other passengers, I would look sideways out of the window at the endless fields of sugar-cane stretching away in all directions. Before long, though, Aunt Esneda would stop me, saying 'It will make you sick!'. Inevitably I dozed off to be woken up only when we arrived at the ancient station in Palmira, the adventure over until the next time.

5

King of the Castle

It is thanks to my cousins that, despite my handicap, I had a fairly normal childhood. They were the same age as I was, and whereas they had the bodies, I had the mind. As far as I was concerned, it was the perfect partnership. Aunt Chela's only grand-daughter, Tania and my cousin Gloria both understood perfectly that they had to do my bidding because I was disabled. What I said went, and I must admit that I enjoyed this power shamelessly. It was I who chose our games and ordered how they should be played. It was I who thought up our naughtiness, and I who was allowed to be rude. But it was Tania or Gloria who got all the blame.

Like most small children, we played Mummies and Daddies. I was always Dad, of course, while Tania or Gloria was my grown-up daughter. I was certainly not prepared to have either of them as a wife! I sat and watched happily as my 'daughter' scurried around obeying instructions. I would order her to get the room into a mess, then tidy it up. Then there was the shopping, cooking, washing and ironing to do, not to mention pushing her old disabled father round in his wheelchair. She even had to force-feed her baby with soapy water. Poor Tania's favourite doll was ruined!

Like most small boys, I was anxious to know how little girls are made. I had such power over Tania that I could make her undress to order. We knew it was naughty but could not understand why. Girls were expected to sit in a lady-like manner, their knees together. Sexual topics and bodily functions were taboo subjects for girls to mention in front of a member of the opposite sex.

I think there is a certain amount of violence in every child. There certainly was in me, combined with a need to dominate and manipulate others to compensate for the sense of helplessness engendered by my useless limbs. I needed to prove to myself that I had some kind of control.

Before Tania and I were old enough to go to school, we would sit together on the porch in Toro, watching the world go by. A poorly dressed, bare-footed little girl used to trot past our house at the same time every day, on her way to buy bread for breakfast. We thought of her as our enemy, because she dared to walk along our stretch of pavement. Strict measures were required. As Commander in Chief of hostilities, I ordered Tania to run out and pull the girl's pigtails. The following morning, we were astonished to see her advancing towards us again. Obviously a new method of attack was needed. Something a bit more violent. Tania was ordered to run up to the girl and punch her. After several of these daily assaults, and many tears from our young adversary, she tried to avoid us by using the pavement on the other side of the street. As my trusty lieutenant had been forbidden to cross the road, this new manoeuvre proved more of a challenge. Finally, after much pondering, I devised a new strategy. The next time our victim trotted into view she was assailed by a rubber shoe. It landed bang on target, hitting her full in the face. We could hardly believe our eyes on the following day when she returned, this time clutching the hand of a tiny brother. I noticed that the boy had a hare-lip, and was not prepared to risk harming another child with a disability. Instead, I commanded Tania to do the unthinkable. She ran blindly across the street, straight through the traffic, and smacked the girl, who burst into noisy tears.

My sense of power was beginning to lose its charm. Although it was annoying, our enemy's refusal to retaliate was stirring hitherto unknown pangs of guilt in me. The girl's helplessness mirrored my own. Thankfully, she eventually described our cruel campaign to her mother, who arrived red-faced and furious, demanding instant retribution. As usual, I was deemed to be completely innocent of any crime, while Tania was whipped hard across the legs with a length of cane from the garden. My sense of shame was not quite strong enough to make me confess my role in the whole sorry business, although I feel rather differently about it today.

One of the greatest challenges to my desire for power arose during a long-running vendetta which I waged against another cousin, Jorge. He boarded with Aunt Chela in Toro in order to attend a sort of agricultural sixth-form college. Jorge was born in

Cali, not in his home town, because of his parents' flight from Toro. During the fifties political rivalry was violent and country towns became strongholds for one party or the other. Outsiders were driven out by threats of death. By the time he reached his late teens his parents decided that he was becoming too much of a handful. They thought agricultural work would help to sort him out, and sent him to live with Aunt Chela, in Toro, away from the temptations of the city.

Jorge's room was at the end of the corridor. As he was often out with his friends he fitted a small padlock to his door to keep out unwanted guests. This padlock, with its engraving of a rabbit's head, became my Holy Grail. I was desperate to get my hands on it and spent many satisfying hours plotting my strategy. As soon as Jorge left his room for the bathroom or the telephone, leaving the precious padlock unfastened, I ordered Tania to grab it. She then hid it behind my back as I sat in my little wooden chair, the picture of innocence. I had won the first round. When Jorge returned and found his padlock missing, he was naturally suspicious but dared not raise his voice to me, around whom the household revolved. Eventually, he complained to Aunt Chela. I was interrogated fiercely but maintained that I knew nothing about the missing padlock. It was only when my aunt began hitting Tania that I confessed. Besides, I knew that as soon as I was moved from my chair the padlock would be discovered, so there was no point in keeping quiet any longer. Jorge had won the second round.

After several similar episodes, I realised that I must adopt different tactics in future. Maybe if I discovered an alternative way of locking his door, he would hand over the padlock. I instructed Tania to get hold of some rope and attach it to the metal rings meant for the padlock. Next I forced her to spend about twenty minutes tying the rope into a succession of tight knots, hoping that Jorge would be so impressed by this new method of locking doors that he would give me the padlock. If not he would at least suffer the punishment of having to struggle for hours to unpick the knots. It had not dawned on me that he had a knife and could easily slice through the rope! Tania and I repeated this rope-knotting performance several times, so that I could enjoy his frustration each time he found his door swathed in yards of rope.

All-out war was declared. Now I ordered Tania to hide Jorge's belongings and soon his possessions began to go missing. His underwear was buried in the compost heap, books disappeared and were found in people's beds, and his precious gym kit mysteriously flew over the wall into next door's garden.

When Aunt Chela confronted and smacked Tania, she denied all knowledge of the missing items. It was only when the neighbours appeared clutching the gym kit that we knew the game was finally up. Poor Jorge – no wonder he had tried to keep away from his two small tormentors. I did not see him again for about nine years, when we had a good laugh over the war of the padlock. I never did get my hands on it.

6

Aunt Chela

My happy world began to collapse when I was six. I was told that my beloved Aunt Chela had cancer of the womb, and might die. She underwent some radiation therapy in Cali, where she stayed with one of her brothers – Jorge's father. When it was obvious the treatment was having no effect, Aunt Chela changed doctors. For a year, she was prescribed capsules containing rattlesnake venom, something which I found mind-boggling. She was forbidden to eat any meat during this time, as apparently it would have clashed with the snake venom and killed her on the spot.

I had never come across death before. I thought people just stopped being alive so I was quite unprepared for the horror of a long-drawn-out illness. We couldn't afford to send Aunt Chela to a private clinic and there was no point in her going into a state-run hospital. In Colombia, they only accept terminally ill patients after receiving money in advance. We had none.

In two years, Aunt Chela changed from a happy, apparently healthy, well-built, middle-aged woman into someone who was sick, subdued, thin and old. Through it all, she clung to her religious beliefs. But as we waited for a miracle her condition steadily worsened.

At the beginning of the second year of her illness, I went to stay with Aunt Chela in Toro. Originally sent there for a month while Mum, Eduardo and Orlando went on holiday to Ecuador, my short visit extended eventually to nine months. Mum and Eduardo's trip was an attempt to patch up their relationship, which was becoming increasingly stormy. It seemed that the more money Eduardo made, the less likely he was to remain faithful. In the event, things between them deteriorated so much that Mum walked out with my brother, and went to stay with Aunt Esneda. With so much upheaval going on, it was decided that it would be easier to leave me with Aunt Chela.

I only realised the seriousness of Aunt Chela's illness when my great-grandmother Felisa, Aunt Esneda and Tania's mother, Consuelo, arrived to stay and take care of both her and Aunt Hilda, who had recently had a hernia operation. The three women rushed around all day like mad things, trying to run two households as well as nurse the sick. I would overhear frenzied conversations about how to relieve Aunt Chela's pain. They used every home remedy they could think of, and it was only when the pain became unbearable that they scraped together enough money to pay for morphine injections.

Throughout her long illness, Aunt Chela never forgot my needs. On her better days she would take charge of the household again and make sure that I was properly dressed and entertained. But, in spite of her best efforts, there were many occasions when no one could spare the time to pay much attention to me. I was often left in my pyjamas, unwashed and untidy, although I was perfectly happy and played contentedly with Tania and Gloria. As it turned out, my dishevelled state was to have dramatic consequences.

During this unexpectedly long stay in Toro, Mum ran Aunt Esneda's household in Palmira and tried to make plans for our future. She felt that taking a menial job must be her last resort – almost anything was better than that. Joining the police force appealed to her and she was offered a place on a course but, as things turned out, she never took it up.

Mum discussed her worries with my real father's sister, Aunt Maria, who lived in Buenaventura on the coast. Maria's other sisters, and her mother, Susanna, had emigrated to London nine years earlier. One day, Maria arrived at Aunt Chela's house without warning. She had obviously journeyed to Toro in order to assess my situation and, equally obviously, she found it wanting. My apparently neglected state shocked her. Soon afterwards, Mum received a letter from grandmother Susanna, saying it was high time that I was sent to live with her in England, especially now that Mum could not afford to pay my medical bills.

Mum was completely torn. She hated the thought of my being so far away from home, with people who were not used to me and whom I did not know. All my Colombian aunts were equally horrified by such an idea. Aunt Chela, especially, was convinced that the English doctors would use me as a guinea pig for their research, and would end up killing me. And, she added, if the doctors didn't manage to finish me off, the cold weather would.

Aunt Chela also knew that if I went to London she would never see me again. A few days later she said to me: 'If I die, will you come with me?' Her idea of the afterlife, of course, was Paradise. Perhaps she wanted me to enjoy it too. We crossed fingers and made a pact, but when Mum discovered our secret she was adamant that I should break the agreement immediately. Aunt Chela said nothing when I told her I had changed my mind.

During the last few weeks of my stay in Toro, I became increasingly aware of the rapid deterioration in Aunt Chela's condition. The cancer had spread to her bladder, causing incontinence. she was fitted with a catheter which kept becoming blocked. I overheard many worried discussions about this situation and the dreadful pain it engendered. It all sounded absolutely terrifying and I prayed hard that I should never have to suffer such an instrument of torture.

Over a year later Mum was to tell me about Aunt Chela's last days. After I had left for London, Mum went to Toro with Orlando. One night, the blocked catheter caused Aunt Chela so much distress that Mum and Felisa ran through the town to find the new district nurse. They discovered her attending the wake of her daughter who had been murdered in a local feud. The nurse refused to leave even though Mum fell to her knees and begged for help. Soon the catheter became so useless it had to be removed. the incontinence could no longer be controlled.

In spite of the strong family opposition, Mum knew that there was really no alternative to sending me away and she braced herself to break the news to me. I remember vividly the day she arrived from Palmira to see me. We sat alone on a bench in the kitchen and Mum explained that, as there was no future for her with Eduardo, we were now very poor. Although she was trying to get a job with the police force, it would mean her going away for a year's training. Orlando would always be provided for by his father, but I would have to live with Aunt Chela, who was dying. If I went to England, the doctors might find a cure for my illness and, even if they didn't, I would still receive the best possible medical care. Without that I should surely die. I listened in shocked silence, then eventually asked if I would ever see Mum or Orlando again. In spite of her reassurances, I doubt if she was very certain of it herself.

Although dreadfully apprehensive, I accepted my fate and even, occasionally, felt quite excited by the prospect of going to a new country and learning a new language. London was the most advanced city in the world. I knew that from watching films – science fiction ones, as I later realised! It had wonderful space-age buildings, with voice-activated doors and video phones. The clean, bright streets were filled with blond, blue-eyed people, and all the cars were Ferraris. Maybe it wouldn't be so bad after all!

The day I was to begin my new life arrived. I was eight years old. My grandmother, Susanna, had sent her twenty-year-old daughter Ester, all the way from London to collect me. She would meet me in Palmira where my mother was staying with Orlando. It was time to leave Toro and Aunt Chela. On the morning of my departure, I was woken up at 4am by great-grandmother Felisa, who was to accompany me in the taxi. She dressed and fed me, then took me into Aunt Chela's bedroom to say goodbye. As I looked at her, lying in the huge bed, her pale face lined with pain, I was devastated. Her silent tears and final words to me only increased my anguish. She wished me all the luck in the world, hugged me tight and kissed me, saying: 'Goodbye, my little *divinitas*. This is the last time I shall see you.'

Desperate to cheer her up, I said: 'I am sure you will get better, Aunt, and then everything will be all right.' She shook her head as the tears flowed faster. By now everyone in the room, including the men, was crying. Only I remained dry-eyed – too shocked for tears.

Aunt Chela died in her bed, shortly after I arrived in London, aged just 44. Everyone who loved her was relieved that her suffering was finally over. Mum told me later that soon after the funeral, members of the family who were still in the house were disturbed to hear an eerie scratching noise coming from the dead woman's bedroom each night. The women lay awake, terrified, until the men came home from the bars. After about a week it was decided that the noise was coming from the bed itself. There was no other

explanation. Mum and Aunt Esneda pulled the whole bed apart
and found, tucked inside a pillowcase, a box of tissues. Written on
it was Aunt Chela's message. It was her farewell to me:

Diego, my life. I know I will never see you again.
May God Bless You.

After that, the noises ceased.

7

Leaving Toro

It was not yet light when my family gathered to wave me off from Toro on the morning of my departure in September 1982. I gazed around the house where I had been so happy trying to remember its every detail – the yellow and white tiles on the living room floor; the square, undecorated, bricks on the kitchen and hall floors; the old-fashioned blue-painted mud and dung plaster walls of the corridor; and the small glassless windows with their wooden grilles, so high up that you had to stand on a chair to see out. I would miss it all so much.

Last of all I caught sight of my beloved Aunt Chela's precious aloe plant. It hung inside the front door, apparently living on air. Like many of her generation my great-aunt believed in the plant's magical power to repel evil spirits and to bring luck to the house-hold. It had certainly failed this time.

Great-grandmother Felisa carried me to the waiting taxi and we waved a sad goodbye. Once on our way I was diverted from my melancholy thoughts by studying Felisa's hands. They never ceased to fascinate me – with their covering of paper-thin skin which somehow held in check a bunch of fat blue worms. Try as I might to push them down, they always popped back up again. The sight of veins so full of blood frightened me. What if one were pierced? Great-grandmother Felisa would bleed to death, and that I could not bear. It was she who had once saved my life by insisting on taking me to hospital when no one else would trust the doctors. Once there, she acted as my nurse for over a week. It was she who had brought me a bedpan when my legs were encased in plaster, and who had given me a record I longed for passionately – a won-derfully maudlin and sentimental ballad about a poverty-stricken little boy who is killed as he runs across the road to pick up a toy thrown down by a rich child. His last words are: 'I'm going to play with Baby Jesus now.'

As we approached Palmira, I was torn between excitement at
the prospect of seeing Mum and Orlando again, and anxiety about
meeting Aunt Ester who was to take me to London. As it turned
out, I had a three month reprieve. Aunt Ester went to stay with her
sister, Maria, in Buenaventrua while Mum gathered together all the
necessary paperwork. This included obtaining my birth certificate,
proof of baptism, Mum's marriage certificates (proof of my
legitimacy), various letters and visas from the Immigration Office
in Bogotà, my passport and identity card and my father's death
certificate.

In order to assemble all the papers, Mum and I, sometimes
accompanied by Orlando, spent many long hours queuing. The
only way to speed things up was through bribery. There was a
further delay when I developed a chest infection, which took three
weeks to clear. Not that my Aunt Ester minded – she was in no
hurry to return to London and was making the most of her
new-found freedom. I saw her only three times before we left for
London, but each meeting was rather formal. We were complete
strangers and it was obvious that she did not relish the thought of
having to cope on a long international journey with her profoundly
disabled eight-year-old nephew. After all, she was only 20.

On the morning after Aunt Ester's first visit, Orlando stubborn-
ly refused to be taken to his kindergarten. He clung to the leg of my
bed, sobbing hysterically and screaming that no one must take his
brother away. His distress upset me because I had always felt
protective towards him. The day he was brought home from the
hospital, a tiny black-haired baby, I appointed myself his guardian
and he responded. He would often wake up at night crying when
Mum and Eduardo were out, and the only way my great-grandmother could comfort him was to put him on my lap, where he
would soon fall asleep. Some of the times when I have felt my helplessness most keenly have involved Orlando. Once I had to endure
watching him being hit by another small boy. I longed to retaliate
on his behalf, but could only give the bully a good hiding in my
imagination. On another occasion, Orlando and I were alone for a
few minutes while Mum went out to the shops. Orlando, then about
ten months old, was asleep, but he suddenly woke up and began to
crawl around the house. He instantly found a cigarette and started

to eat it. I was beside myself, quite convinced that he would poison himself and die. Our next-door neighbour, hearing my panicky screams, peered over the garden wall and tried to reassure me, but I couldn't relax until Mum came home. My mortification was complete when both my Mum and the neighbour had a good laugh at my expense.

Orlando had to be convinced that I was not leaving Colombia just yet, so that he would agree to return to school. Departure day was finally set for New Year's Eve 1983. My mother was to travel with Aunt Ester and myself as far as Bogotà. After that Ester and I would continue on our own.

I remember clearly the bleakness of that Christmas, but there were wonderful moments. On Christmas Eve, Eduardo collected Orlando to take him to a party. In Colombia, children believe they receive their presents from Baby Jesus. My small brother returned late in the evening, laden with parcels, but meanwhile I had gone to bed with a heavy heart. That year Mum could not afford to buy a single gift, and it seemed that Baby Jesus would be leaving me nothing. But in the morning I awoke to find that I had not been forgotten after all – Mum had divided up the spoils. When he was older, Orlando shared his presents with me of his own accord, so we would both benefit from whatever he received from Eduardo.

The end of December arrived all too soon. All the family travelled to Palmira to see me off. Eduardo came to say goodbye and took Orlando away. Once again I was surrounded by sobbing relatives as Mum, Ester and I got into the car which was to take us to Cali Airport. As we drove off I watched as Great-grandmother Felisa and Aunt Esneda crossed themselves, tears pouring down their cheeks.

8

From Bogotà to Ladbroke Grove

On the flight from Cali to Bogotà, Ester ignored me and made small talk with Mum. This continued as we waited five-hours at Bogotà for the flight to Madrid. For most of that time, I occupied myself by looking at the other people in the airport and trying not to think of what lay ahead. At last it was time to board our plane. Suddenly, I felt the whole world was collapsing around me. For the next hour I clung to Mum, my head buried in her shoulder, and sobbed. It felt as if I were being torn in half. The airport authorities allowed Mum to carry me on to the plane: tearfully she placed me on my seat in the middle section. In spite of strenuous efforts to appear grown-up in front of my fellow passengers, I could not stop crying. All I wanted was to go home.

When Mum had gone Ester muttered a few words of comfort, but made no attempt to touch me. As the plane taxied down the runway and took off, I managed to control my tears and tried to think positively about my adventure. I reminded myself that I was in a huge jet, and that I was going to a wonderful city, full of fantastic cars, all the latest technology and happy, smiling people. What's more, I was going to meet a new branch of my family, with lots more aunts who would look after me as my aunts in Colombia had done. Never had my natural optimism been more misplaced.

Although the sadness kept returning, I worked hard at ignoring it. The air hostess gave me some Disney playing cards which I gazed at for a while, then Ester fed me and, after watching some of the film, I fell asleep. It had been a momentous day, made all the more exhausting by the struggle to keep a check on my emotions. I knew that if I really gave into them, I would find it almost impossible to pull myself together again.

I woke early in the morning, desperate to go to the toilet. My bladder felt as if were going to burst but I felt awkward about asking Ester, who was more or less a complete stranger, to take me to the toilet. After hoping for a while that the feeling would go away, I had no alternative but to say as politely as possible, 'Aunt Ester, I really have to go to the toilet, please', adding hastily, 'but only to wee.'

'What am I supposed to do about that?' she asked impatiently. Feeling foolish, I suggested that she could either ask for a bottle or carry me to the toilet. She began to mutter to herself in English, and although I did not understand a word of it at the time, I certainly got the gist of what she was saying: clearly I was a complete nuisance. She picked me up awkwardly, as if I were a sack of potatoes, letting my head dangle so low that I could feel saliva trickling up the back of my throat into my nose, making it sting. As I clung on I was so overcome by embarrassment and guilt at causing such a scene that I even forgot my discomfort.

When we reached the toilet I was horrified. It looked hardly big enough for one person. Suddenly I found myself being lowered on to one of Ester's knees as she knelt on the floor. Supporting my head and shoulders with one arm, she began to fumble with my zip. When at last she found what she was looking for, she rolled me sideways towards the toilet, saying: 'Hurry up and get on with it. I can't hold you for much longer.'

The whole thing was ridiculous. My aunt obviously had no idea about helping small boys with their aim; a great fountain of urine shot out in all directions. Ester's curses became so voluble that I stopped in mid-stream. For the first time in my life, I was feeling self-conscious about my disability. An unusual feeling hit me – the overwhelming desire to be independent.

Relieved that apparently it was all over, Ester hurriedly pulled up my zip and bundled me back to my seat, where I sat in damp silence. Immediately a dreadful realisation dawned. I had to go again. I prayed: 'Dear God, please get me to London soon. I'll never be naughty again if I can just lie down and use a bottle.'

I whispered nervously to my aunt that I needed to go back to the toilet. With a huge disgruntled sigh, she snatched me up and stalked back down the plane to the inappropriately-named convenience. This time I managed to complete my mission. What a relief! It felt good to be alive again. Once back in our seats, I felt encouraged enough to make a concerted effort to endear myself to my aunt. I chatted away in what I thought was my usual captivating manner, asking questions about her family and her home, but her monosyllabic replies and stony expression left me in no doubt that some people really were immune to my charms.

Things did not improve during long stops in Madrid and Paris where Ester again made clear her irritation at my utter dependence. Sweating with fear as I felt her struggling with me and our luggage, I imagined the consequences if she lost her grip. I envisioned a curious crowd gathered round a small, limp body, gasping in horror at the stream of blood pouring through its shock of black hair.

I decided that I really hated travelling, especially by air. There was so much discomfort and fear added to which I had experienced quite new and unpleasant feelings of self-consciousness and embarrassment. How I resented that.

In spite of my misgivings, Ester and I eventually found ourselves nearing the end of our epic journey. I dismissed my angry thoughts and began to look forward to seeing my grandmother and her three other daughters, all of whom I had met briefly when they visited Colombia. The only member of the household I had never met before was my grandmother's second husband. Living with this family, I imagined, would be similar to my happy experiences at home. Really, I assured myself, I had nothing to fear.

On leaving Customs, I saw a crowd of relatives waiting to welcome me. After much embarrassing hugging, I was put into my wheelchair and taken outside for my first sight of Britain. What a shock! It was New Year's Eve, and freezing. We all squashed into the car which, strangely enough, was not a Ferrari! I peered curiously out of the window into the foggy twilight. The airport looked almost the same as the one in Cali, except much larger. The roads seemed dark and uninteresting. As we drove through the suburbs of London I began to feel disappointed. Where were all the hi-tech buildings and the sleek limousines? All I could see through the gloom were rows of identical houses, with peculiar pointed roofs, streetlights that glowed a sickly orange, and small square cars with not even a decent pick-up truck amongst them. It was awful!

We arrived 'home' in Ladbroke Grove, at that time a slightly run-down area of west London. My grandmother and her daughters lived in a council flat on the second floor of an endless brick building which I looked at in astonishment. I assumed that it was unfinished, because the bricks were bare and unadorned with either paint or plaster. There were rows of black doors with not a soul sitting outside them. In fact, the whole place was quite deserted, and looked like a prison.

When my grandmother opened the door to my new home it revealed the smallest hall I had ever seen, completely empty except for a steep flight of wooden stairs. I immediately wondered how strong they were – as ever, I was alert to the possible dangers around me. Whoever it was that picked me up was not at all prepared for my floppiness and I became more and more nervous. Each loud creak convinced me that I would be dropped down the stairs at any moment.

To my amazement, we made it safely into the flat, and I found myself sitting on a folding metal chair in the corner of a dark room. The women all disappeared to question Ester about her holiday in Colombia, and at first I thought I was alone. As my eyes became used to the gloom, I saw a tall, heavily-built ginger-haired man sitting on a sofa in front of the television. This was Peter, my grandmother's Scottish husband. He said 'Hello' to me, but as neither of us could speak the other's language, that was the full extent of our conversation.

Some time later, I was moved into the kitchen where the women had begun to prepare food for a New Year's Eve party. I was quite used to sitting while women worked around me. It also gave me an opportunity to observe my new-found family. My eldest aunt, Teresa, was twenty-five, divorced and pregnant. Ester, who was twenty, came next, followed by nineteen-year-old Ismania and finally Luz, who was fourteen. My father had been the only boy.

When my aunts went off to get changed, leaving me with my grandmother, I realised how alone I was and how much I missed my mother. I rested my head on my arm, in the hope that Grandmother would not see me crying. Suddenly she delved into the fridge and produced a bag of huge prawns, and waved it proudly at me. Unaware that I was supposed to be delighted at the sight of this rare delicacy, I said: 'Oh, those. We had them every night when Eduardo took us out.' I could not understand my grandmother's furious reaction. Even now, more than ten years later, she still remembers my ingratitude!

Soon, the first guests arrived. I sat in the doorway and watched the dancing becoming more and more frenetic. Although exhausted after one of the longest and strangest days of my life, I insisted that I was quite happy whenever the subject of bedtime was raised. I dreaded being left alone in a dark room, visualising myself being pinned to a bed by a blanket, unable to move and sweating with discomfort. I knew that, even if I shouted at the top of my voice for someone to come and rearrange me, no one would hear me above the din. Eventually, Grandmother and Peter decided that enough was enough, and put me into a single bed next to theirs. A drunken Ester later collapsed on to a mattress on the floor.

After saying my prayers, I fell asleep. As usual, every now and then I would call out for Mum to move me. Somehow I have always managed to do this automatically, without waking myself up. There have been nights when poor Mum has had to move me ten times or more, while I sleep peacefully on. Grandmother, on the other hand, was understandably none too pleased by a disturbed night, although her grumbles seemed most unfair to me. No-one had ever complained about my needs before.

The following morning, I woke up in more ways than one. Instead of being the powerful ruler of a little kingdom, my needs now came a long way down everyone else's list of priorities. They seemed to regard me as a nuisance and an embarrassment. The whole family was engaged in clearing up after the party. Eventually I called out, asking if someone could get me up. After a shocked silence, Grandmother shouted: 'Be quiet and wait your turn. Can't you see we're busy?' It was the first time I had been spoken to in that manner. As I lay waiting it dawned on me, at the age of eight, that my childhood was over. I had left behind me the happy cocoon of unconditional love. From now on I would have to 'fend' for myself.

An hour later, Grandmother, Ester and Ismania arrived to give me a bath. Unable to take my T-shirt off, they slit it up the side. It had been Orlando's, and a cherished link with home, but they ruined it. The bath felt very strange and slippery – most unsafe, in fact. I wondered if I dared to say that I had never been in one before. In Colombia I would sit on a special chair under the more common shower. Now I swayed about, terrified of falling into the water. However, as soon as I opened my mouth to speak, I was told to stop fussing and shut up. Once dressed, I was put into my chair and told to eat breakfast from a small, unsteady table which wobbled alarmingly. The rest of the day I spent watching the unintelligible television, sometimes talking to someone for a few minutes. On the wall opposite me hung a watercolour portrait of my father. I gazed at it, wondering about him. Often I tried to steer the conversation round to him in an attempt to find out what he had been like.

For the first two weeks of my new life in England, I was left in bed in the mornings until Luz got up. She was still on her school holidays, whereas all the adults left early for work. She appeared at about 9.30 to dress me, struggling impatiently to force the clothes on to my floppy body. Then she put me in my usual chair and left me there while she gazed dreamily out of the window or spent hours chatting on the telephone. Time dragged, but I kept telling myself not to be babyish. In order to become more mature, I would have to put up with such things without complaint.

Ismania, who worked as a waitress, came back each day at about 1.30, later to return to the restaurant for the evening shift. Of all the sisters, she was the most detached. Ignoring me as much as possible, she would do something for me only if her mother ordered it. Later on in the day, Grandmother would return from her cleaning job. She was especially bad-tempered when she came home from work, and everyone gave her a wide berth until she went into the kitchen to cook the supper. Another meal for me to cope with!

Grandmother had told me that I must feed myself from now on –
not an easy task with muscles which refuse to work properly. At
that stage I still had some use of my arms which allowed me to
stab solid food with a fork, but soup and rice were quite another
matter. Sometimes the meal lasted for over an hour and, even then,
half of it ended up on my lap.

During the dreary evenings I listened to endless conversations in
Spanish about the relative merits of vacuum cleaners and mops, the
cost of London Transport, and the depressing social lives of my
aunts. Whenever the subject matter became more interesting they
broke into English, much to my frustration. Peter worked away
from home, returning only at weekends. Perhaps his presence
would have helped, even though we spoke different languages.
Later on, when I knew him a little better, I realised that both of us
were outsiders – cuckoos in the nest.

At 8.30 every evening, Grandmother issued the dreaded order:
bed! This was the signal to set off for the bedroom, 10 metres away.
I would obediently start pushing round the huge wheels of my
oversized wheelchair, trying to gain some control with weak
sweaty palms. Inch by inch I crept up the narrow corridor, which
was covered in slippery, polished lino. Lying in wait for me was the
terrifying staircase. In order to negotiate the bedroom door, I had to
wheel myself to within 4 inches of the top stair and then make a
90-degree turn. Every night I struggled to block out the image of a
small, broken body at the foot of the stairs.

Half an hour after I had started, I would reach the bedroom,
damp and exhausted. Only then was I allowed to call Grandmother,
politely announcing my arrival. She would come in, undress
me roughly and put me into a ghastly garment she had found – a
pair of towelling trousers covered in flowers. I reflected that if
Tania could see me now I should lose all power over her in an
instant. I lay in the dark, waiting for Grandmother and Luz to come
to bed.

Grandmother was becoming increasingly angry about her
broken nights. When I called out she shouted: 'Shut up! Nights
are for sleeping.' For her maybe, but for me sleep was impossible
unless I could turn over regularly. Too frightened to say anything

more, I would embark on a long struggle to get comfortable. At that time I could still, with enormous effort, move my limbs a little.

After saying all the prayers I knew, I became a sort of slow-motion tadpole, wriggling and squirming about to shift the heavy, restrictive blanket. Without its weight I found it easier to carry out the next procedure. This was to slowly gather up one leg of my pyjamas until I could get my hand under the hem. Then I tugged the leg over and hope my whole body went with it. On good nights, this was a success. On bad nights, my body refused to co-operate and I was left like a beached whale, although by this time I was so tired that I often fell asleep for a couple of hours before waking up and having another go.

One terrible night I woke up, aware that I needed to go the toilet. I had supposedly emptied my bowels that morning, and was certainly not expected to want to go again so soon. Although I used my 'bottle' every day, I usually needed to be toileted only once every three days, and even then my aunts would fight with each other to avoid taking me. I suffered agonies of humiliation when I heard them yelling 'It's your turn!', 'No it's not! You do it.' It was bad enough during the day but I knew that waking them up in the middle of the night to do the hated chore would be much worse. I told myself that I could hang on until the morning but after about five minutes I realised that this was impossible. I began to moan softly to myself, and ended up in tears, waking Grandmother, who demanded to know what was wrong with me now. Despite my desperation, I was unable to confess. It seemed so shaming. Impatiently, she shouted: 'If you won't tell me, be quiet, or I shall have you put on a mattress in the living room.' By this time all I wanted was to get away from her, so I begged to go. Luz was made to carry me into the living room. She closed the door behind her as she left.

I could control myself no longer, and my cries got louder when I realised what I had done. Ester was awake by now, and she and Luz came into the room. When they discovered the mess, they carried me to the bathroom, quarrelling and swearing. They tore off my underclothes and threw them in the rubbish bin. Their exclamations of disgust added to my embarrassment. When you are eight years old and your toileting has always been done by people who love you, it is hard to understand reactions like these. Finally, washed and in clean clothes, I was put back to bed. At least darkness provided some cover for my shame and humiliation.

9

My Father's Family

Although I often felt frightened of my relatives, life seemed quite different when they were being pleasant to me. I was desperate to be liked and, at the first sign of friendliness from them, I found it easy to forgive everything. Each time I told myself: 'Now it will be different. I can start again with a clean slate.'

On my first weekend in Britain, Grandmother and Aunt Teresa took me to the local market, where they bought me some plastic toys and a teddy bear. I was overjoyed, because surely this was a sign that they liked me at last. I was full of optimism for the future.

What they did not tell me at the time was that they had bought me the presents so I would have something to play with when Luz went back to school and I was left alone each morning. Until then, I had never been left by myself for more than an hour in my whole life and I wondered how I could possibly cope. However, I told myself that it would be unreasonable to make a fuss and that it would not get me anywhere if I did. This was the way life was going to be in England and I must accept it. It was still a frightening thought, made much worse by the imagined prospect of 'ghostly visitations'.

Each morning, before she left for school, Luz helped me to use the bottle, then gave me a grilled cheese sandwich for breakfast. She left the radio on in the kitchen and made sure that I had a box of toys on the bed as well as some peanut butter sandwiches for lunch. The toys were my only consolation.

From the time that Luz left until Ismania came home, at about 1.30, I lay in bed looking at the ceiling or at one of my toys. I often tried to will Ismania to come home quickly by imagining her route back, counting her footsteps. She may not have had any time for me but she was definitely better than a ghost! The sound of the radio, which was meant to soothe me, only increased my anxiety. What if it were masking sounds made by the ghosts? I should have preferred to have been able to hear them coming down the corridor to get me, rather than lie in bed and wonder where they were.

Boredom was never a problem – I have always managed to live in my imagination when necessary. Each time I wanted to do something I worked out a plan of campaign. If I felt like playing with a toy the only way to reach it was to walk my reluctant fingers slowly across the bed, curl them around it and carefully pull it back towards me. I used the same technique when it was time to eat my sandwich. Because of my limited movement, that little exercise often took up to an hour and a half.

As soon as Ismania arrived, I forgot the loneliness and fear of the morning. She would get me dressed, and put me in my usual chair in front of the television. I was quite happy now, and looked forward to the rest of the family coming home. It was only when I was in bed again that I would began to think about the dreary morning to follow.

This routine went on for weeks. Nothing changed except, occasionally, the filling in my sandwiches. Instead of peanut butter it was jam or cheese. However, there was one break in the routine which I could have done without. One morning I reminded Luz that it was my toileting day, and that I would like to try to go now, please, before she left. She screwed up her face in disgust and told me to hurry up, or she would be late for school. I became too nervous to manage anything and she hastily put me back to bed. I begged her to leave a potty and some toilet paper on the floor, where I could reach it if necessary.

About an hour later my worst fears were realised. I needed to go to the toilet, and I broke out into a cold sweat wondering how on earth I was going to do it. Slowly I rotated my body until I was lying on my back, my legs dangling. I wriggled forward until my bottom was positioned above the potty. Everything went according to plan until it came to using the toilet paper. To my horror, I saw that somehow it had rolled across the floor. What on earth was I going to do? I managed to slide the potty to one side and drag my pyjama trousers up. My strength ran out and I was stranded. I did not have the muscle power to haul myself backwards on to the bed, and I was frightened of sliding forward and cracking my head on the hard floor. As I felt the panic rise, I caught sight of my teddy.

Gradually I pulled him towards me, then pushed him off the bed, praying that he would land in the right place and act as a cushion. I am not sure if it was thanks to God or to my clever calculations, that teddy landed in exactly the right spot. As I slid off the bed, my head fell backwards straight on to the waiting bear.

The relief was so enormous that I was quite euphoric, until I began to consider the consequences of this horrible episode. It was bad enough having my bottom wiped in the usual way, but it would be much worse this time. Perhaps things would not be so awful if I got the potty out of the room. I started a long process of shuffling along on my back, clinging on to pieces of furniture as I went. At the same time, I pushed the potty forwards whenever I could. Eventually, we both arrived in the corridor, about 3 feet from the stairs. There was no more I could do – the bathroom door was closed and I was exhausted. I lay in the corridor for the next two hours, hoping fervently that I had tried hard enough to make amends and earn a pardon. But it was not to be. Ismania complained bitterly when she found me, and refused to give me a bath until Ester arrived to help. Another set of my precious underwear was thrown out, and by the time I was clean and sitting in my chair watching television, I felt thoroughly crushed. However, perhaps my punishment was justified. I was eight years old and still not able to control myself. Maybe I deserved the humiliation.

When you are disabled as I am, the daily management of bodily functions assumes major importance, and my greatest dread was that such an event would happen all over again. And it did. This time I was left alone in my usual place in the living room while all the family were out at work on their various shifts. Once more the dreaded sensation came over me. The effort of trying to prevent another ghastly accident reduced me to tears. As I looked desperately around the room, I caught sight of my father's portrait. Perhaps it was an omen. When I narrowed my eyes and peered through the tears he looked all blurry. I decided that, if I could detect him smiling out of the distorted image, everything would be all right; if not I was doomed. The answer soon became clear and I had disgraced myself again. Aunt Teresa, who did not live at the flat, arrived to collect something. To my utter surprise, she took my predicament in her stride. Although very pregnant at the time, she somehow got me into the bathroom and cleaned me up, chatting in a friendly way all the time. I was full of relief and gratitude, but my happiness evaporated the moment Grandmother came home and heard the news. I watched in horror as her face flushed red and her eyes seemed to bulge in contempt as she stared at me cowering in my chair. Suddenly she reached forward, dragged me out of it, and marched into the bedroom, where she threw me down on the bed, pulled down my trousers and smacked my bottom, threatening me with 'the belt next time'. No one had ever laid a hand on me before. I felt a mixture of anger, embarrassment and despair, but a strong sense of self-preservation prevented me from showing my feelings. Before long, I was able to chat to Grandmother as if nothing had happened.

I think she was determined to bend me to her will, just as she did with her daughters. She seemed to believe that my illness was psychosomatic, and that if she stopped treating me like a small child I would regain the use of my limbs and run about like any able-bodied boy. At weekends I was forced to sit up at the kitchen table for meals. The slippery plastic chairs were very narrow and without arms. With nothing for me to hold on to, I sat in terror, hardly daring to breathe in case I lost my balance. Trying to eat at the same time was out of the question – I was convinced that I would fall off the chair and crack my head open.

I was not always treated harshly by my surrogate family. I am grateful to my grandmother for taking me to my hospital appointments, which often involved long periods of hanging around while waiting to be seen. At Paddington Green Children's Hospital the orthopaedic surgeon decided that I needed a brace. This was to be quite unlike the uncomfortable contraption I had left behind in Colombia. The English doctors wanted me to get used to it slowly, so I was first fitted with a brace made from stiff foam rubber. I wore it every day for about six months before I was given a plastic version. I received physiotherapy in an attempt to prevent my limbs stiffening up.

We also had to attend the Maida Vale Hospital, where a specialist monitored my chest condition. My lack of mobility, and the wasting nature of my disease, means that my chest has always been very weak. I had to undergo all sorts of tests, one of which I will never forget. Two needles, linked to a big box covered in scary-looking knobs and dials, were stuck into various parts of my body. This was made worse by the fact that, at that time, I spoke barely any English so had no way of asking or understanding what to expect. Grandmother, this time accompanied by Peter, was just as unprepared. Suddenly, the doctor pushed the needles into me and turned a knob. My leg jerked violently as a huge electric shock whipped through it. My screams of agony and pleas for him to stop fell on deaf ears and, if anything, seemed to spur the doctor on to activate all my other leg muscles. Finally, my cries in Spanish, begging for an end to this torture, had an effect. Grandmother and Peter took pity on me and insisted that the test should be stopped immediately.

After a while, life in Ladbroke Grove settled into a routine. Grandmother ruled the roost and my aunts did as they were told. Only Luz had problems in coming to terms with her duties. At first, I missed Mum all the time, but gradually my home-sickness subsided and I succeeded in putting her out of my mind except when I got into trouble. Then, I longed for her. I wrote her a few letters but knew that they would be read before they were posted, so I could not tell her how things really were.

Now that I no longer had to use every ounce of energy on survival, I became aware of the increasing friction between Grandmother and Peter who spent more and more of his time away from the flat. Grandmother seemed to be even more crotchety and short-tempered than usual, and became particularly impatient at what she thought was my lack of effort. She was now convinced that I had been so pampered in Colombia that I had a psychological resistance to walking. So she devised a plan that would put her theories to the test – I was going to get downstairs on my own.

One evening, my aunts were sent to the launderette as a punishment for coming in late the night before. Grandmother sat sewing while I watched her. Out of the blue, she announced that it was time for me to learn to tackle the stairs by myself. I was speechless with terror and disbelief. She put me into my foam rubber brace and sat me on the top stair, saying: 'Now, get to the bottom.' Terrified, I peered down the staircase which held so many fears for me. My trousers were made from a slippery fabric and the stairs were varnished wood. One false move, and I would hurtle down like a sack of potatoes.

My tears had no effect and Grandmother said: 'I'm leaving you here for fifteen minutes. When I come back you will be down the stairs.' I prayed hard, asking God to help me, but was unable to move although I managed to get a weak grip on the banisters. When Grandmother returned she pushed at my bottom with her foot. I flopped down on to the next step, where I sat crying, telling myself that I must be really wicked to deserve such punishment. There was nothing I could do to help myself. If I fell to the bottom I should surely die. Another fifteen minutes passed, and I heard Grandmother's footsteps coming back along the corridor. She pushed me again, and I slid down another step. And so it went on. Each time the build-up of fear increased until I told myself I could not take any more. I tilted myself backwards so I could slide down gently, but suddenly I was hurtling down the stairs. I came to rest half-way down, on a step that was larger than the others, and lay there screaming with panic. Grandmother ran down and picked me up, declaring that I was no better than a useless rag doll. Once more she threw me on the bed and threatened to hit me with a belt for being such a coward. By now I was sobbing with terror, and she stood watching me in silence for a minute before putting the belt away and charging out of the room. I heard the key turn in the lock and wondered how she thought I might be able to make an escape.

Still, I was happy to be alive and intact. While it was probably my very floppiness that had prevented serious injury, I was convinced that *God* had answered my prayers.

My presence in the flat had not gone unnoticed. When Grandmother applied for a resident's visa on my behalf I had the first of many encounters with officialdom. A social worker came to visit and then contacted the local authorities about schooling for me. Apparently there were no spare places in the local special school, so I was to be sent temporarily to a home for mentally handicapped children.

After breakfast each morning, Luz dressed me in her usual sadistic manner; then pushed me to the special Centre before going on to her own school. I spent most days sitting with one of the three adults who worked in the home. The resident children were sent off to school each morning in a bus. Not yet able to speak English, I found it a lonely existence. The staff tried to be friendly, but I felt isolated and out of place as I sat and stared at the wall charts in the office, or looked out of the window at the people going by.

One day I found myself alone in the television room when a youth of about sixteen appeared. I looked in astonishment at the large heavily-built young man with the dark beginnings of a moustache on his upper lip. Placed firmly on his head were his underpants. I watched, petrified and helpless as he suddenly began to tear around the room banging his head against the walls. Just as I was convinced he was about to attack me, two members of the staff rushed in to restrain him. After that, the long periods of boredom did not seem quite so dreary.

Probably because I was much easier to deal with than their usual children, the staff became quite attached to me. Often during the day the young woman would push me to her room to listen to records, or one of the men would drive me somewhere interesting, such as London Zoo or Buckingham Palace. Yet, despite these attempts to make my life more interesting, I actually found myself longing to be back in the flat. All my life, my greatest joy has been to talk to anyone who will listen, so not being able to communicate properly with the staff in the home was hard to bear.

It was usually Luz who came to collect me after school each day. Her resentment of her new duties became more and more evident. She knew I was terrified of falling over or out of my chair (which had no seat belts), yet she would wheel it along the very edge of the pavement, laughing gaily at my polite requests to walk along the centre. One day, the chair's wheels wobbled so much on the kerb that I was flung sideways and landed with my chin resting on the bumper of a parked car. Amazingly, I was only bruised and shocked. Luz scooped me up, insisting that I was not to tell anyone. Not that they would have believed me if I had – they would have accused me of being a baby, as usual.

Luz soon developed another form of torment when she realized that the wheelchair-wobbling could result in her getting into trouble. When we arrived back at the flat, she would leave my wheelchair in the hall, having first pulled my coat off and hung it up. On good days she carried me upstairs without complaint, but when she collected me from school in a bad mood, I knew what to expect. After wrenching off my coat, she would lift me up by my knees, so that I dangled upside down and my head banged against each step. If I cried, she shouted at me, so I learned not to react. I think I was more frightened of a verbal battering than of physical pain.

Luz also revelled in her power over me when it came to my language lessons. Once I began to spend time outside the flat, the family decided that I would have to learn English, so someone bought me a diary. A list of English words was written down as each day's entry, with a Spanish translation beside them. I had to memorize these words correctly or face my punishment. This depended on the mood of whoever was testing me. Mistakes usually resulted in another fierce telling-off, but Luz preferred to hit me with a ruler, provided no one was watching.

Looking back on it, I suppose that, as a fourteen-year-old girl, Luz was thoroughly fed up with having to care for a crippled eight-year-old who could do practically nothing for himself. Grandmother was very strict, and no doubt her daughter was venting her frustration on me. Even so, I can never forgive her for her cruelty. She is the only person I have ever truly hated.

A lot had happened by the summer of that first year in England. I had been taken to various hospitals, was being treated by specialists and had undergone numerous tests. But all this took time, energy and money. Eventually my new family had had enough of all the hard work involved in caring for me. They decided to send for my mother.

Phone calls and letters flew back and forth across the Atlantic. By now Mum had a part-time job as a secretary in a furniture factory opposite Aunt Esneda's house. Although Mum and Eduardo lived apart, he still collected Orlando from kindergarten each day. He then spent the afternoons driving around, visiting shops and banks on business, with his small son sitting beside him in the truck. Like all Colombian men, he revelled in showing off his male offspring.

One bedtime, Mum told Orlando that she had to leave him to go

to me, but that he would soon join us in England, unless we came
back to Colombia first. Orlando asked 'why can't we just get Diego
back?' Mum explained that she could no longer afford that.
Grandmother Susanna in London was paying half her air-fare, and
the furniture would have to be sold to pay the rest. Orlando would
go to live with his own grandmother because Eduardo now lived
with a new girlfriend, and Mum could not bear the thought of her
son being with them. Aunt Esneda was unable to help because she
too had developed cancer.

10

My Mother Arrives in London

When I knew that I was actually going to see Mum again I hardly dared to show my excitement, determined not to leave myself open to ridicule or disappointment. Having listened to endless adult conversations I knew it was possible that, as she was not a resident of the European Community and a Columbian to boot, Mum might be questioned for hours at the airport and, even then, refused entry. I was sure that, if that happened, the family would mock me. I had to protect myself so, struggling hard to appear nonchalant and mature, I refused to go to the airport to meet her.

Finally, it was the day of Mum's arrival. I wondered if she would notice any changes in me after seven months. I watched my grandmother and aunts get ready to go and meet her, and told myself sternly that they might return without her. I would not believe she had arrived until I saw her with my own eyes.

When at last I did see her, I felt strange. Part of me wanted to hug her and burst into tears, but I also felt strangely shy. I had learned to hide my feelings and needed to appear grown-up in order to save face, although I was actually bursting with happiness and relief. Surely now I would be out of their clutches? I couldn't wait to tell her about all the goings-on of the past few months.

Mum was startled by the change in me and even impressed by my rather restrained and detached attitude. When her sisters-in-law invited her to a Colombian night-club that evening, she accepted, thinking that as I was now so grown-up, I would not mind. But I did. I minded terribly and longed to beg her to stay. I spent yet another evening watching television with my grandmother.

The following day, Mum was informed that I was much more mature now – the implication being that I had been a spoilt baby when I arrived from Colombia. I really resented that. Mum was so amazed at how polite and quiet I had become that she even began to feel guilty, thinking that perhaps she had not been a good mother by always letting me say whatever I wished, even to the point of rudeness. She was also amazed at my self-sufficiency. Whenever she tried to help me eat or brush my teeth, I moved away saying: 'No, I can do it.' I was worried that they would find out Mum was helping me and tell her that I was lazy.

On her second evening, Mum stayed at home and the rest of the family went out. She chatted to me, trying to find out how things had really been. I told her a little, but felt unable to really unburden myself. Mum was so indebted to her mother-in-law for taking me in that I dared not disillusion her all at once. Besides, I did not want her to think I was telling tales about my grandmother's family. As it turned out, however, she soon saw how life was at first hand.

Mum was allocated a rather hard single bed in my grandmother's bedroom. By now I was used to struggling to move myself around during the night. Once again alert to my needs, Mum woke at once as she heard me fighting with my bedclothes. She whispered 'Are you OK?'. I couldn't help replying that no, I wasn't, so she tiptoed over to sort things out. The noise disturbed Grandmother, who shouted at her to go back to bed and to stop wrapping me up in cotton wool.

Gradually, I became more dependent on Mum again and felt able to tell her about the way Grandmother and my aunts had treated me. Within a week of her arrival, she knew virtually everything.

I think she was more astonished than anything else, yet she was also embarrassed. For example, my grandmother made me brush my teeth, even though it could take over an hour for me to do so. Mum had never even made me try, and I think she felt guilty about that.

Before long, Mum had turned into an unpaid servant. Her deep sense of obligation meant that she cooked and cleaned all day long. Grandmother revelled in this and became quite tyrannical. She showed no gratitude when Mum brought her slippers the minute she came in from work each day and expected her to perform other menial tasks as well. In fact, her need to dominate became so strong that she forced Mum to take me to church each Sunday, even though no one had bothered about this before. Actually, we soon started to look forward to the peace of those Sunday mornings, away from the inhospitable and cramped flat.

Ladbroke Grove is very near Notting Hill, where a carnival is held each August Bank Holiday weekend. The floats passed in front of the flat, and Grandmother insisted that I should watch. She put me into a sort of deck chair and placed it on top of the 2-foot-high wall that surrounded the balcony. The wall was very wide but I was terrified. The whole family knew that I was afraid of heights, but it made no difference, even when I begged to be taken down from my perch. They told me that I was being a baby yet again, and needed the discipline that this experience would give me.

My cries brought Mum rushing out. She scooped me up in her arms and carried me to safety oblivious of the scorn emanating from everyone else.

Even though I might have enjoyed the carnival under any other circumstances, I barely noticed the colourful floats passing by – all I could think about were the possible consequences of a gust of wind catching my chair.

As usual, Luz proved to be particularly adept at upsetting me. I found myself once more in her tender care when Mum took on two cleaning jobs. By now Luz had stopped maltreating me physically, and was concentrating all her efforts on teasing or shocking me instead. One day, she returned from a biology class and treated me gleefully to a horribly graphic and embarrassing lesson about sex. I could hardly believe my ears. Was this really how babies were made? It sounded revolting!

The next illusion she shattered was my implicit belief in Baby Jesus's generosity each Christmas. My crestfallen reaction was everything she could have wished for.

When it was Luz's turn to join the cleaning contingent, I had to spend two hours a day by myself again. It was a blessed relief to be left alone, although Mum was racked with guilt about it. She struggled to save as much of her wages as possible after paying Grandmother for our keep. Still not yet twenty-five, Mum rather naïvely believed that the English doctors would cure me, so that we should be able to return to Colombia and Orlando. When she discovered that my brother was now living with Eduardo and his new girlfriend, her determination that we should return home increased. In the meantime, in London, my education became a priority.

11

Starting School

There were no schools for the disabled in Colombia and the family could not afford private tuition. I was now eight years old and had never been to a proper school. Aunt Chela and Mum had taught me to read and write in Spanish, and I had picked up some of the rudiments of maths from Tania and Gloria, who used to give me lessons on a toy blackboard when they came home from school.

My social worker finally managed to find a place for me in the nearest school for the disabled. I was delighted. Now I would be really grown-up – I was joining the big league at last. I had learned enough English to make myself understood, so I waited, full of confidence and expectation, for my first day at school.

Mum returned from her early morning cleaning job and got me ready, complete with packed lunch, a note book and pencil. At 8.30 the school minibus sounded its horn and I joined several other children on board. The driver introduced himself and we set off.

The Franklin D. Roosevelt School was a revelation – it was the first building designed especially for the disabled I had ever encountered. The other children were taken off to their classrooms, and I was met by a smiling woman who said her name was Mrs Jenkins and pushed me off to my classroom. We went down wide, cheerful-looking corridors which were well-lit by large windows. I was interested to see that all the doors opened in both directions. Later on, I discovered spacious, well-equipped rooms for specialist subjects – a computer room with excellent facilities for pupils with communication difficulties, toilets designed for children with varying needs, and the medical department which was always staffed by a nursing sister. It was like being in another world, and I loved it.

Mrs Jenkins introduced me to Dorothy, my teacher, and to my nine classmates, most of whom were also in wheelchairs. When I saw them, realization dawned. 'I am one of those,' I thought. Until that moment, I had never really regarded myself as disabled, just a late starter, as my great-grandmother had said. I suddenly knew that there would be no instant miracle. If ever I were to walk it would be a slow and painful process. Even now I refuse to give up all hope, although I am incapable of moving any part of my body except for three fingers on the left hand. But, at the age of eight, I came to terms with the fact that I would spend my life being labelled 'disabled' – a term I now dislike intensely. To say that I am handicapped or crippled is much closer to the truth.

My new teacher was very friendly. She often had us all laughing and let us use her first name. Yet, strangely, whenever I expected to be helped straightaway, she would become rather cool. She was teaching me to wait my turn, a concept which was entirely new to me – I continually forgot that I was in a classroom with other children of similar needs. Dorothy would shout 'wakey, wakey!' if we were not listening, and it impressed me so much that I followed her example when I wanted her attention. That was when I discovered that adults in the outside world could not be spoken to in the same way as they spoke to children! Until I went to school, I had not been used to much structure or discipline. Swearing was the only thing truly frowned upon in my family. Yet, now, saying 'wakey, wakey!' to a teacher was apparently a shocking thing to do. It was very confusing.

My next teacher was quite different. Mrs Altoft was tall, attractive and somehow completely in control. She was friendly but kept her distance, and expected nothing but the best from her pupils and their attendants. As a result, we always knew exactly where we stood with her, and lessons were stimulating and original. For the first time in my life, I felt that my mind was being stretched, and I revelled in my newly-acquired knowledge. Mrs Altoft was also practical and made things as easy as possible for us to work properly. My favourite attendant, Pam, contributed to my contentment. She listened carefully to my instructions when I needed to be made more comfortable, and never objected to doing my toileting. I looked forward to school every day.

During the holidays, Mrs Altoft ran the play centre. The children had the run of the school, and there were special activities or school journeys each day. Her teenage nephew, James, used to come along to help, and he and I became firm friends. I enjoyed his company much more than that of my contemporaries, with whom I felt I had little in common. They all wanted to play with their Action Man toys, whereas I was much happier practising the noble art of conversation.

Mrs Altoft's kindness to me went way beyond the bounds of duty. Months later, when Mum and I had eventually moved to south London, she and James used to drive across town to collect me first thing in the morning and take me to the play centre, even though I was no longer a pupil at the school.

12

Family Rows and Finding New Friends

My life became a constant see-saw of highs and lows. In the Spring I was sent with my classmates on a journey to a place called Sayers Croft – a wonderful country centre for schools. I was thrilled to be able to join able-bodied children in some of the activities. I returned home, full of excited stories about my holiday. To my horror Mum told me that she, too, needed an break and was going to Scotland for a few days. Quite irrationally, I felt completely abandoned.

While Mum was away a letter arrived for her. My grandmother read it of course before handing it over. Mum was mystified by the cold reception she received on her return from Scotland until she read 'I'm so sorry that you are having such a bad time with your mother-in-law'.

The next day Mum handed over our weekly rent (to Grandmother), who snapped: 'No, don't pay. Just find somewhere else to live.'

Mum replied: 'All right, I will, but please allow me some time to find suitable accommodation for Diego'. At this Grandmother exploded. 'You needn't think you're taking *him* anywhere. He's staying with us.'

Mum found this ridiculous, and said so. Grandmother was quite unused to having her authority challenged, and shouted that it was she who was responsible for the future of her son's child.

I had been fast asleep, oblivious of the stormy row taking place in the kitchen, but I was jolted awake by the sound of Grandmother screaming: 'Get out of my house! But there's no way you'll take Diego with you.'

I lay in bed, my heart racing. What was going on? Then I heard Mum's voice, high and strained. 'I'm sure there are laws to protect my rights as a mother.'

'People like you, who are illegal immigrants, have no rights here. If you try anything, I'll report you to the authorities, and you'll be sent back to Colombia to starve,' Grandmother retorted.

'OK! Go ahead. But I'll still take Diego. I'm certainly not leaving him here to be killed off by you.'

There was a stunned silence. My heart began to pound as both women burst into the bedroom. Mum looked at me, 'Describe all the things they did to you, Diego – like the time she made you crawl downstairs.'

Although by now I was rigid with fear, Mum's presence reassured me slightly. Suddenly, I felt as though a valve had been released – at last I could let out all my pent-up feelings. Shakily at first, I related all that I could remember of the cruelties inflicted on me during my first months in London. Grandmother listened in shocked and embarrassed silence. I watched her face flush a deep red until she shouted: 'You're just as much of a nasty vicious little viper as your mother. Anyway, it's all her fault that you're a cripple. She didn't feed you properly. What you're suffering from is malnutrition.'

I looked nervously at Mum. As far as she was concerned, this was the ultimate insult and I wondered how on earth she would react. I half-expected her to hit Grandmother, but instead she yelled: 'How dare you say that, you mean old cow! I'll take my son away and I don't care if you never see him again.'

Now that Grandmother looked as though she was going to cry, I felt quite triumphant. In spite of my terror at ending up in prison, waiting to be sent back to Colombia, there was immense satisfaction in being able to hit back at Grandmother through Mum. After a brief silence, Grandmother flounced out of the room. Although it was some time before we actually moved out, neither she nor Luz spoke to us again for over three years.

It was a strange time. As we began our frantic search for new accommodation, in one way I rather enjoyed the feeling that it was Mum and I together against the world, but the stress was hard for her to bear. She must have felt isolated and alone in a country where she could not speak the language. Each day, after school, we wandered around Notting Hill Gate or down the Portobello Road, looking at the shops. I still found it astonishing to see fruit and vegetables lying unattended on racks outside the shops. In a Colombian city, everything would have been snatched at once by small hungry hands. I stared in amazement, too, as people chose the food, then put it into paper bags and went inside the shops, actually demanding to pay for it!

From my vantage point in the wheelchair I looked up at the crowds passing by. Everyone seemed to be in a hurry and what a strange mixture – white, black, Asian, Chinese. There were Rastafarians with huge cascades of tangled hair and crazy-looking punks sporting brightly coloured cox-combs on their shaven heads. As for their clothes! In Colombia, they say 'You can always judge a person by his suitcase'. That certainly did not seem to be the case in London! Here people actually seemed to choose to look like walking jumble, with large holes in their trousers and baggy, worn-out sweaters!

The cars were almost as bad. I gazed in astonishment at so many battered old bangers. Anyone in Colombia lucky enough to own a car, treats it with tender, loving care, however old it might be. I thought of the gleaming 1950 Chevolets covered with often useless status symbols – huge extra headlights, enormous tyres, protruding mirrors and flashy new upholstery. As we struggled along narrow, uneven pavements, I would gladly have been back sitting next to my hero, Eduardo, as he roared up and down the streets of Palmira in his beloved pick-up truck.

Sometimes Mum and I stopped to gaze into one of countless antique shops. How extraordinary it seemed to us that people actually chose to pay out huge sums of money for such old stuff, instead of advertising their wealth by buying the most modern of everything. As for spending a fortune on a single used stamp, a pile of old cigarette cards or a collection of useless coins – the very thought of such extravagance made Mum furious!

At least it was easy to find something to eat during our enforced walkabouts. I quite enjoyed our picnics in Kensington Gardens, although the lack of public conveniences sometimes caused a problem. Once I became so desperate that Mum had to rush off and buy a carton of drink, which she then poured away. I lay on a bench struggling to use the carton, only too aware that Mum was upset by our being reduced to such indignities. I felt pretty foolish and fed up with myself. London is not an easy city in which to be wheelchair-bound.

Every so often we would meet Esperanza, a friend of Mum's, who was staying at Aunt Teresa's flat. She was also having problems. Her biggest worry concerned the possible loss of her student visa. The two friends talked for hours about their various predicaments and decided to share a flat. Most of the landlords they met were only too happy to rent accommodation to two attractive young women, yet when it became clear that I was part of the package, an extraordinary number of obstacles suddenly materialized out of thin air. Some landlords trying to be polite mumbled excuses about narrow corridors, steep stairs or possible obstructions. Others took one look at me and announced that they were not prepared to upset their existing tenants by my presence!

Eventually, Esperanza found a room on her own. Mum and I looked forward to visiting her, but we had not bargained for the landlady's attitude. When she saw me, she said to Mum: 'You can come in, but not him. The wheelchair will ruin my carpet. Leave him outside.' As I listened to this, I thought 'Perhaps I should be tied to the railings like a dog'. At least then I would not lower the tone of the woman's rather shabby block of flats. It was hard to get used to adults being so bigoted and ignorant. I was used to children saying I was rather a big baby to be in a pram, too lazy to walk, or looked peculiar. They didn't know any better, but with adults, it used to be different.

This was an enormously difficult time for Mum. It looked hopeless. We would never find anywhere of our own to live because no one was ever going to put up with me. It must have been doubly infuriating because she spoke little English and had to rely on me, a nine-year-old child to act as interpreter. She often cried and even talked about committing suicide, although I'm sure that was classic Colombian over-dramatization rather than anything else.

Mum missed her family in Colombia terribly and the tense situation in the flat only increased her sadness. Orlando, at this time was still living with Eduardo and his new girlfriend. Each day he took his son to see Aunt Esneda, who was by now in the terminal stages of cancer. Eduardo felt it was his duty to visit her, because she had been so kind to him and Mum when they were living in poverty during their early years together. Esneda's husband worked for the town council and was often sent to work a shift at the local abattoir. In the past he used to bring home cheap pieces of meat and offal for Eduardo, Mum and me, and Aunt Esneda had often lent them money which she could ill afford.

Orlando enjoyed these visits and happily answered all Aunt Esneda's questions about his home-life. She would pass his replies on to Mum whenever she rang.

One afternoon, Mum felt particularly homesick. We sat on our usual bench in the park while she prayed over a picture of Christ sent to her by a friend in Colombia. 'I need to talk to someone who understands,' she said, so we set off for the nearest public telephone box to ring Aunt Esneda.

Just as we found one, I looked up to see two people walking towards us. I recognized the woman, a Colombian called Holga, who had worked at the holiday play centre. She introduced us to her husband Michael. This chance encounter was to be the beginning of a change in our fortunes. Holga said to Mum 'I can't help seeing that you are upset. Can we help?'

Mum was thrilled to hear a sympathetic voice speaking to her in Spanish. Soon, we found ourselves in a large bed-sitting room. My wheelchair was left out in the passage, while I sat on a comfortable sofa. Mum poured her heart out to our new-found friend, describing our desperate search for somewhere to live. From that day, despite the fact that their landlord did not allow them to entertain visitors, Holga and Michael's room became our refuge. We went there almost every evening for supper. At the time, Michael was an unemployed bricklayer so money was scarce, but they were happy to share what they had with us. Nevertheless, Mum never arrived without some kind of contribution towards the meal, which she also cooked. While the three adults talked I watched television whenever there was enough money to feed the electricity meter.

Michael introduced us to a solicitor. Although Mr Goldberg specialized in business law rather than immigration, he wrote a letter describing our circumstances. This we were to give to whoever ended up representing us. He also suggested that the best place to look for help would be my school. I felt thoroughly inspired

by a man who possessed such wisdom combined with the ability to
protect people. As there was little chance of me becoming a famous
general who could defend my country against its oppressors (my
previous ambition), I immediately decided to settle for being a
lawyer.

Mr Goldberg endeared himself to me even more by treating me
as an equal. He listened patiently to my efforts at meaningful
conversation and gave me confidence in my ability to communicate. It was a completely new experience. Although Colombian
children may be dearly loved and even listened to, most adults
assume that they talk nonsense and their ideas are dismissed as
being childish. But Mr Goldberg thought me sensible enough to
take on the responsibility of fighting for our cause. I was now the
man of the family.

The next day, at school, I tried to suppress my secret fears. If
I told someone about our predicament what could go wrong? What
if things got out of control? What if the authorities discovered
all sorts of irregularities and made matters worse, not better?
However, there was nothing else we could do, so I waited behind at
lunchtime and spilled the beans to Mrs Altoft. She took me straight
to the headteacher, a kindly woman with whom I empathized
because she had one leg encased in callipers and wore a heavily
built-up shoe on the other. I recounted my story once again.

13

On the Move

There was nothing that the social worker could do unless Mum was granted some form of citizenship. Although she had now been in England for almost a year, she had postponed making an application. It was as much as she could do to look after me and to tolerate living in our hostile home. 'All I can suggest is that you find some friends to take you in' were the social worker's final words.

While we waited, with considerable apprehension, for our future to be settled, Mum and I continued to visit Holga and Michael. Sometimes, so as not to impose on them too often, we would visit Aunt Teresa instead. Up until now, because she lived in her own flat, she had remained on the sidelines of the battle between Mum and the rest of the family.

One day, towards the end of the summer, we visited Teresa's flat. Mum had written a long letter to Aunt Esneda, bringing her up to date with all our latest news. Two or three hours later, we were back in Grandmother's flat preparing to go to bed. Mum was in the middle of putting me on the toilet seat when she let out a shriek. 'Oh, my God! What's happened to Aunt Esneda's letter?'. A horrified look flashed across her face. 'If I left it in Teresa's flat, I must get it back before she finds it. Sit there. I'll be back in a few minutes.' With that, she tore out of the toilet, slamming the door behind her.

I clung on. My splints, which stuck out in front of me, began to hurt my legs and I broke out into a cold sweat. I was not only too frightened but also too proud to shout for help, so I struggled to keep my balance. Panic-stricken at the sight of the closed door in front of me, I tried to talk myself into remaining calm by visualizing Mum's movements. 'She has only been gone for a few moments,' I told myself. 'She must be coming up to the post-box by now. Only another short walk and she'll be back.' Half an hour later, I was in despair and in such a state of shock and exhaustion that, when Mum finally did appear, I could hardly speak.

The moment I saw her face I knew that the worst had happened. Teresa had read the letter in which Mum had written: 'I can do nothing. The old cow is making our lives hell.'

Mum described the scene as she ran towards Teresa's flat. Her sister-in-law was waiting outside, holding the offending letter and shouting: 'You stupid ungrateful bitch! After all we've done for you! Luckily for you I won't tell my mother until tomorrow. And then you'd better leave before she chucks you into the street.'

'We've really had it now,' Mum told me. 'It's the end. I don't know what to do. We'll just have to leave.'

After putting me to bed, Mum went out to the nearest phone box to ring Albel, a young Colombian ex-boyfriend of Aunt Ester's. He worked as a waiter at a local restaurant and Mum and I had often chatted to him at the flat while he waited for Aunt Ester to get ready. Albel was only eighteen but he seemed much older. He reminded me of Eduardo, with his generosity and gift of the gab. But it was his flair with women that impressed me most: his ability to court the daughter by charming her mother had almost reached an art-form. He and his brother had even taken us on a day trip to the Isle of Wight, and we had been invited to his sister's wedding where the whole family treated us with kindness.

Albel was sympathetic but said regretfully: 'I really don't think you can come and live with us. As you know, Maria, my sister, is here. Because she came over from Colombia after she turned eighteen, she is living here illegally. We cannot risk being found out before she gets her visa. But don't worry – I'll try to fix something with my other sister. Just hang on for a bit.'

The following morning, Mum left early for work. I heard Ester moving around in the kitchen. When Mum returned in time to get me ready for school, she was greeted with a torrent of abuse from the young woman.

'How dare you write a letter like that, you miserable creature!' Ester yelled. 'All Mum has done is help that bloody child.' I listened in horror. In Colombia, it is very shocking to swear about a child – it is almost a blasphemy. While Mum controlled her urge to hit Ester, my aunt continued: 'You've got exactly ten minutes. Get out!

As soon as Mum gets back I'll tell her everything, then she'll get on to Immigration.'

Mum flew into the bedroom and dressed me in double-quick time. Then she grabbed all our belongings and thrust them into black bin-liners. Festooned with bundles, like a bag-lady with a pram, Mum was standing on the pavement outside the flat as the school bus sounded its horn. She retreated behind a pillar, pulling me with her. She had no desire to be seen in such a state. The bus left. I did not go to school again for over six months.

As we looked at each other, wondering what on earth to do next, the local council road-sweeper came along. We had exchanged greetings with him before, so now Mum plucked up the courage to ask him for help. She quickly told me what to say and, as usual, I did the talking in English. The friendly West Indian readily agreed to look after our belongings, including my commode attachment for the toilet. Everything was pushed into his store cupboard, and we set off for the phone box once again. Mum got through to Albel who said he was sorry, he hadn't had a chance to talk to his sister yet, but why didn't we go over to see him anyway.

We had made the journey to his flat in Tulse Hill, south London, several times before, but now Mum was worried and agitated. When it came to changing trains at Stockwell tube station, she was so distracted that she stepped on to the extremely steep up-escalator without positioning my wheelchair properly. A terrible few minutes followed, while Mum struggled to prevent my chair from toppling back down the escalator. As I looked anxiously up to the distant top stair, I felt the two front wheels of my chair wobble precariously. All I could hear were grunts and sighs, and then Mum muttered: 'It's no good. I don't think I can go on holding you. You're going to fall at any moment.' The further we progressed up the escalator, the longer the fall would be. I braced myself, hoping desperately that one of the people rushing up beside us would notice our plight and help. Just as Mum's hands were finally losing their grip, we reached the top of the escalator. She wheeled me off and for the next few minutes sat silently on a nearby seat, in a state of collapse. I thought how different things would have been in Colombia. No woman would have been left in such obvious difficulties there, especially one as young and attractive as Mum.

At long last, we arrived at the block of flats in south London. Albel opened the door in his underpants, because he was on a late shift that day and was catching up on his sleep. He installed me in the living room in front of the television, then went back to bed. Mum was already very late for the start of her shift as a chambermaid, so she left too. When Albel's mother arrived back from her early morning cleaning job, she found me happily ensconced in her flat. Without questioning my presence, she made me some sandwiches and then proceeded to trot back and forth through the flat, carrying a variety of boxes and bags.

When Mum returned and recounted our story, Albel's mother told her that our room was ready. She had been clearing out the store room for us. It was small, cold and dark, with only a single bed which had lost two legs and was now balanced on a tower of rubber tyres. We were to share the room with various boxes, a laundry basket and two wardrobes, but at least we had some privacy and thought ourselves very lucky to have been made so welcome.

Little did we know then that this would be our home for almost two years. We shared the flat with Albel, who had his own small room, his mother, sister and her son. The flat was on the second floor of a block in a big, rough council estate. It was quite a struggle to get my wheelchair up and down the stairs, but all the family were prepared to help and no one ever complained about the tight squeeze we caused in the flat. By now I was nine, so I enjoyed having another child to play with. John was seven so Albel's sister must have been very young when he was born. There was no father on the scene.

Before long, my manipulative instincts got the better of me and John became my legs, running countless errands, however mischievous, without question, even on the day when I ordered him to shoot all the ornaments on the mantelpiece with my toy gun!

My lack of physical ability had taught me very early on to devise suitable methods of dealing with resistance.

A quick curse was enough to get John moving but it was not always so easy. A small boy sometimes visited the flat with his mother. For some reason he took a deep dislike towards me. Delighted to discover that I could not retaliate, he pinched my arm until it bled. My curses only spurred him on to bite as well. One day I noticed my tormentor's terrified reaction to the sight of a feather boa in the wardrobe. That was the last time he attacked me. On each future visit he was confronted by the bright pink, fluffy snake sitting protectively on my lap!

14

Mrs Garner and Our Own Home

Although I watched John setting off for school every day, I never wondered why I stayed behind in the flat. I simply accepted my fate, and sat in front of the television, watching everything from Tom and Jerry to the Open University. After about six months of this, a social worker from the local authority came to see us. Someone must have informed her of my situation. I told her that we didn't know of a suitable local school for me, and I was quite sure that I would be beaten up if I went to John's school. All the boys seemed so rough.

Two weeks later, I found myself sitting in a taxi on the way to a local school for the physically disabled. I felt rather resentful, convinced that no school would ever be able to match up to Mrs Altoft's. My fears were confirmed the moment I was wheeled through the entrance. The building seemed small and poorly equipped compared with the Franklin D. Roosevelt. It was obvious that there were no wealthy parents to support this school.

I gazed in dismay at my fellow pupils. They were all so obviously disabled that my heart sank. Yet again I was forced to face my own short-comings, and I could not stop the refrain running through my head: 'You are like them, you are one of them, you look just as weird.'

When I was small, my Colombian aunts had told me: 'You will go to school one day: other boys will look after you and push you about and take you to meet all the nice girls.' I had nurtured visions of being the centre of attention, easily able to cope academically, never lacking the assistance of an able-bodied friend. Now I had to face the thought of being anonymous – of being herded together with these children. Surely I was not really like that? I watched them – some grinning stupidly, others jerking their limbs convulsively or even dribbling. Why couldn't I go to a normal school? I wouldn't mind a bit being the only disabled pupil. I look back in shame at such unworthy thoughts.

Someone pushed my wheelchair into the school library. This was to be my classroom. I felt awkward at meeting the teacher and my classmates, who were much older than me. I supposed that they would judge me by my appearance, just as I had done with them. But there was nothing I could do about it. A few days later I became a pupil at the school with which I was to have a love-hate relationship for the next six years.

Mum's solicitor advised her that the time had come to complete the formalities for her application to stay in Britain. She and Albel's married sister, Jennifer, who was to act as interpreter, went to see the solicitor. He helped Mum to sort out a few problems which lingered from our stay with Grandmother. A few weeks later, Mum was summoned to the Immigration Office near New Scotland Yard. No one was available to translate for her, so she took me. After a fruitless search for a Spanish speaker to sit in on the meeting, the Immigration officer told me that I would have to interpret and that I must translate every word exactly.

He interrogated Mum for over an hour, often asking her the same questions in different ways. To help our cause Mum suggested that her application should be treated favourably because, had he not died, my father would have certainly brought us over to England in due course. We were horrified to learn that in fact he had never mentioned having a wife and son in his own applications for residency in Britain.

Eventually, we were allowed to leave and heard nothing more from the Immigration Office for several months. Early one morning, everyone in the flat was fast asleep, having been out late the night before at a Colombian club. Only Albel was up, polishing his prized new car. He nearly fainted when two official-looking men, both carrying briefcases, walked towards him. Albel was worried that they had discovered the illegal status of his younger sister and was relieved to discover that they had come to see me and Mum. After a second interrogation lasting over an hour, they told us that we now had the right to stay in the country while our papers were

being processed. It was to be four years before we were granted
residency.

Now that we no longer felt like criminals in a foreign land, my
main preoccupation was school. The bus arrived at 8 o'clock each
morning, and I was always its first passenger. The driver was
cheerful and funny, and the attendant was a jolly Italian woman
with whom I immediately felt at home. We picked up children
along the way, and arrived at school at about 8.45. Attendants
waited in the school entrance hall, ready to transfer us from the
bus to our electric wheelchairs so we could whizz off to our classrooms.

In my class, the specially adapted desks were ranged round the
teacher's. Those children who could not write had their own elecrtic
typewriters. I was still able to move my hands and arms then,
albeit very slowly, so I had one too. At ten, I was two years
younger than most of my fellow pupils, but I felt quite happy and
able to hold my own. Lessons were challenging and I revelled in
competition. I also got on well with the teacher and the attendant,
who worked as a team.

I struck up a special friendship with the physiotherapist. On my
first day at the school, I was taken to the physiotherapy department to be met by a tall, attractive, middle-aged woman who took
one look at me and said to her colleague: 'I'll have this one. I like
the look of that mane of black hair!'

Although I sensed at once that we would get on well together, I
had no idea how much Mrs Garner was going to mean to me. After
assessing my needs and enquiring about the treatment I had
received at the Franklin D. Roosevelt School, she asked me about
my family and life at home. While Mrs Garner stretched out my
limbs, trying to ease the stiffness, we talked non-stop. Within a few
days, she knew my whole story. I looked forward eagerly to each
session with my new friend. She was such fun to be with – always
sympathetic, but also matter-of-fact and firm. I can remember
thinking that she was exactly the sort of wife I would like when I
grew up!

At the approach of colder weather I developed one of my chest
infections. Mum usually waited for them to go of their own accord,
and did not ask the doctor for antibiotics, but this time it was

different. My temperature soared and I began hallucinating. Albel insisted on taking me to hospital in his car, and we waited for over an hour in the casualty department of King's College Hospital while I struggled to breathe and Mum became increasingly anxious. Within minutes of the diagnosis – pneumonia – I was lying in the children's ward, attached to a drip.

When I went back to school, I told Mrs Garner all about my stay in hospital, which had turned out to be rather enjoyable surrounded as I was by people and attention! She told me she was sure the pneumonia had been brought on by the damp in our bedroom. 'We'll have to get you re-housed,' she announced.

Two days later, she drove Mum and me to the housing office in Brixton. We joined the long queue, which stretched out of the door and into the street, and prepared ourselves for a long wait. It was intensely cold and, as soon as she noticed how miserable I was becoming, Mrs Garner pinned on her badge which said 'Senior Physiotherapist' and confidently pushed me to the front of the queue, shouting: 'Excuse me, please, this is urgent.'

The man behind the counter had no choice but to keep quiet while she talked. I listened with an admiration which later increased when she obtained in record time the necessary medical certificates from my specialists. Mrs Garner also arranged registration with a GP and would often accompany me to hospital appointments in order to monitor my treatment.

After two years of living in the cramped but friendly flat with Albel's family, we were given our own accommodation. There was absolutely nothing in it but at least it was ours. On the ground floor, it had a living room, kitchen, bathroom, large toilet and two bedrooms. The doors had been widened to accommodate a wheelchair. Mum and I slept on a mattress while we collected together suitable furniture with Mrs Garner's help. Mum cleaned and decorated and soon our flat felt like home. At long last, we were no longer guests in someone else's house and, most importantly, we were in a position to return some of the hospitality our friends had shown us over the past two years.

During the school holidays, Mum took me to Mrs Garner's house in Dulwich, in south London. It was an enormous bungalow, beautifully furnished, and with en-suite bathrooms. I had never

seen anything like it! I met her husband Eddie, who was also in a
wheelchair and she told me how they had met. As a young man, he
was a talented sportsman who had been invited to enter a rowing
race on a river in India. The boat capsized and Eddie contracted
polio, which paralysed him from the waist down. He was sent to
the Royal National Orthopaedic Hospital in London, where he met
his wife who was then a newly qualified physiotherapist.

I could talk to Mrs Garner about anything. When the subject
of sex came up, I told her how much it worried me because of my
disability. I could not see how I would ever manage. She smiled
and said: 'Just look at Eddie and me. We have two children, so it
can be done.' I was to remember those words when I felt self-
conscious in the company of girls.

I grew to love and trust my self-appointed surrogate Granny.
During the school holidays she gave me physiotherapy either in her
own home or in our flat. One winter there was thick snow outside.
It was bitterly cold, and I was too ill to go out. The bell rang and
there stood Mrs Garner and her dog. They had walked 3 miles to
see how I was. Actually, she became so involved with me and Mum
that I have a feeling the other staff at school resented what they
saw as favouritism. Even so, Mrs Gardner's kindness changed our
lives, and her influence and guidance have stayed with me.

Mrs Garner had been an integral part of our lives for four years
when she retired. Her time was occupied more and more with her
family, especially the two grandchildren. We began to lose touch so
I was delighted to see her once again at a school concert, although
I was quite unprepared for her gaunt appearance. She casually
mentioned that she had been having stomach pains.

Less than a year later, I was attending an art lesson when the
teacher, Nick, asked me to wait behind so that he could speak to me
in private. At break, the two of us went out into the playground,
and Nick told me that my beloved Mrs Garner was dead. I went
completely cold – it was like losing Aunt Chela all over again.

The following week, Nick took me to the funeral. I was the only
pupil from the school to attend. Mrs Garner was cremated – a
horrible idea to me. It seemed so final. At least if the body were
buried, it would mean that something of her would be left. After
the funeral, we all went to a big hotel for a buffet lunch. I found it

all very different from the Colombian way of death, in which the dead person is the centrepiece of the proceedings. After the priest has said the last rights, the family lays out the body dressed in its Sunday best. Apparently asleep, the body then lies in state in the middle of the living room, surrounded by candles. The family and friends, dressed in black and with the women in veils, hold a 24-hour vigil. Mourners clutch rosaries and light candles. The room is filled with the sound of prayers. Every now and then someone reminisces about the deceased and triggers off another session of sobbing, wailing and prayer-chanting.

Food is provided throughout the night, and at about 9 o'clock in the morning, the male relatives and friends, followed by a procession of mourners, carry the coffin to the church for the funeral service. Then the coffin is carried to the cemetery and buried, to the sound of loud and anguished farewells. The very rich hire *mariachis*, groups of musicians who look like Mexicans with their round black hats, black suits and cummerbunds. They play suitably mournful music on their guitars and sing of broken hearts and death, in order to ensure a satisfyingly emotional send-off.

As I gazed around at my fellow mourners, I wondered at their restraint and stiff upper lips.

15

Art, Philosophy and Intimidation

Mrs Garner gave me emotional, spiritual and physical support, but it was my art teacher, Nick, who became my intellectual mentor. The first time we met was on my introductory tour of the school, and I was impressed by his evident enthusiasm for the efforts of his pupils. It was plain that this quiet, unassuming man in his early forties really loved his work. What is more, his pupils responded to his commitment by giving him their attention and trust.

During my first lesson, Nick asked me what my interests were. I replied: 'Fast cars and fighter planes.' He asked me to draw something, and thoroughly approved of my illustration of a futuristic car complete with wings! Over the years, I invented all sorts of amazing contraptions, almost none of which could possibly work in practice. My enjoyment came from being able to express my ideas, no matter how bizarre, without being ridiculed or told off. Nick took my extraordinary designs seriously, explaining patiently why they were unworkable. He never fell into the trap of so many other teachers who pronounced that things were wrong without giving a reason.

My English teacher was absent for half a term, and Nick was asked to fill in. I loved those lessons, which mostly consisted of listening to stories. When I missed them because of frequent chest infections, Nick suggested that I go to see him during my lunch-hours to catch up. That was the beginning of a special relationship which is still going strong. After lunch, I would drive myself straight to the art room, which became the venue for deep discussions on all sorts of subjects.

Nick lit many sparks in me. It was through reading *Animal Farm* together that I learned about politics and the difficulties of making the socialist theory work in practice. I realized that it is not human nature for everyone to consider other people's interests. At the time, Nick was very keen on Wittgenstein, and this rubbed off on me. In fact, I rather fancied myself as a philosopher. We used to have heated debates about religion – he was an agnostic, I, am a believer. In the end, we agreed to disagree, but I learnt a valuable lesson – that everyone is entitled to his own beliefs and that, if I were to learn anything at all, I must listen to other points of view before making up my mind. Nick helped me to accept my life, although I had never really questioned why God had made me the way I was. It was His will, and perhaps even bad things happen for the best.

At one point, I became enthralled by the subject of mythology. If Nick was not in school, I spent the lunch-hour with his colleague, Mr Sullivan, who was an authority on the subject. After reading some books, I returned to Nick, eager for further discussion. He allowed me to express my point of view, but was also quite prepared to let me know when I over-stepped the mark. My naïve attitude towards art – that it was all a bit pointless – soon changed. Nick explained the symbolism in early paintings, and I learnt to look at them with new eyes.

Occasionally, we were taken to the National Gallery, which was quite a performance with a classful of disabled children. I loved these visits, and made the most of the opportunity to display my newly-acquired knowledge. Once I hogged the limelight so much by answering every question asked by the education officer that he suggested I might like to take over the talk! Later, I asked Nick if he minded my showing-off. 'No, go ahead,' he replied. 'At least it shows we're teaching you something.'

Sometimes I managed to persuade Nick to describe his own early life – his childhood in Manchester and student days at art college. I listened, fascinated, to his tales of the sixties, complete with flower-power, long hair, short skirts, pot smoking and LOVE. I came to the conclusion I had been born thirty years too late!

My close relationship with Nick did not go unnoticed, especially by some of the attendants who seemed to resent me for receiving special treatment. In due course, it led to trouble.

I had a new bus driver, Jock. One day, on his radio I heard news reports of the latest IRA bombing. In an attempt to make conversation, I said: 'England is such a brilliant country but it's a shame there is so much terrorism here.'

Edna, my new attendant, looked appalled, then furious. 'If you don't like it here, then why don't you go back to your own country?'

All sorts of bitter feelings rose up in me. During the last twenty months I had heard almost daily complaints from my relatives about exploitation by English bosses, who apparently paid little and expected slavery in return. It seemed to me that foreigners were welcome in Britain only if they did the work no one else wanted to tackle and accepted their meagre wages in grateful silence.

Remembering those conversations and thinking about the ever-present threat from the dreaded Immigration Department left me feeling vulnerable, not to say paranoid. I reacted instinctively. 'What do you mean, you stupid cow?' I howled. 'Without us bloody foreigners there would be no one to clear up after you. Anyway, if you English took a few more baths, maybe you would clean yourselves up.'

All hell was let loose. Edna, her face purple with fury, shouted: 'You horrible cheeky little kid. I'll get my sons to come and beat you up.'

A fleeting vision of two enormous thugs bearing down upon me, a small crippled child in a wheelchair added to my swirling emotions. Jock tried to make me apologize, and eventually I squeezed out a few grudging words, but the damage had been done. I was now cast as a troublemaker and must be taught to toe the line. From then on, my time at the school was overshadowed by both fear and resentment at what I felt to be unfair and cavalier treatment.

A few days later the school bus was late so Mum and I went back into the flat out of the cold. When we heard the horn and returned to the street we were greeted with a torrent of abuse from Jock and Edna. Even my apologies made no difference, only provoking a stream of complaints throughout the journey. On our arrival at school Edna reported my apparently appalling behaviour to the school secretary who joined in the outrage. By now I was late for my lesson. Edna grabbed me and practically dropped me into my electric wheelchair. My foot twisted and I cried out in pain. She snapped: 'Stop moaning. Don't you ever stop complaining?' My ankle swelled up and throbbed for the rest of the day. I wondered whether Edna thought that, because my legs were useless, they felt no pain.

There were many such incidents to follow. In a way, they might seem rather trivial, but for me they assumed huge proportions in their cruel confirmation of my utter helplessness.

It was quite ironic that the person I most disliked was the one I was forced to rely on. I began to dread asking Edna for help, but I had no choice when it came to things like taking me to the toilet. She was not too cross when I only wanted a wee but, when it came to anything else, I knew I was in for it. I had trained myself only to open my bowels when I was at home, and had become pretty good at hanging on. However, there was one day when I knew this wasn't going to work. By the time I had plucked up enough courage to ask Edna to take me to the toilet, it was almost the end of the lunch-hour. The whole business could take half an hour, and Edna told me: 'It's far too late, and I can't manage you on my own, anyway.'

In despair, I drove myself off to the computer lesson, struggling to suppress the ever-increasing urge, which by now felt as though it had taken over my whole body. Unable to concentrate on anything else, I soon began to feel dizzy and sick. During the afternoon break, I again begged Edna to take me to the toilet. She replied: 'No, there's no time now. Besides, it's only an hour and a half until you get home.' Before long, I was forced to tell the teacher that I was ill – I couldn't move. Somehow, I managed to hang on, sitting in a sweaty daze. When she put me on to the bus to go home, Edna whispered to Jock: 'You'd better get going. Diego has some urgent business.' They both dissolved in laughter. By the time I arrived home, I was groaning uncontrollably. From then on, I made Mum get me up half an hour earlier each morning to ensure that I was never put in that position again.

By now, Jock had clearly joined the conspiracy to keep me in my place. At one point, we had to use another bus while our usual one was being repaired. It was very small, with an old-fashioned lift which came up to form half the floor. I was put in last, so the front wheels of my chair straddled the join between the ordinary floor

and the lift. As we neared our destination, Jock lowered the lift by
an inch or two. I clung on as hard as I could to the arms of my
chair, desperately trying to conceal my terror. When we arrived,
Jock parked the bus, walked round to the back, opened the doors
and jerked the lift tauntingly until I was convinced I would topple
over. The road was only 2 or 3 feet below me, but that gap could
have been the Grand Canyon as far as I was concerned. I listened to
Jock's chuckles as he finally let me down on to the pavement.

Edna's next ploy was to target my life-saving visits to the art
room to see Nick. She began to waylay me in the playground,
insisting that I must leave him alone during the lunch-hour. 'How
dare you think you can go to see him every day like that, wasting a
teacher's time?' I changed my route but Edna soon got wise to that
and made sure she walked past the art room window in order to
catch me inside with Nick. More tellings-off ensued, until I had
a brain-wave. All Nick's stores were kept in a large walk-in
cupboard. I would make straight for it as soon as I got to the art
room each day. Once inside, I could no longer be seen from the
window. After watching my strange behaviour for some days,
Nick's curiosity got the better of him. 'You must have seen everything in there by now. What's the big attraction?' he asked.
Out came the whole sorry saga of my persecution. Nick listened
carefully and promised me he would speak to Edna about it. After
that I was allowed to attend our daily discussions in peace, but the
verbal attacks continued.

I know that I did not fit into the required mould. My extended
Colombian family had given me a strong sense of self-worth. For
them, my disability made me special, even superior – mentally, at
least – to my peers. But in this school I was being taught that I
must not speak out for myself. It seemed that, when the teacher
was not there, the attendant was the one who should decide what
my needs were. I had no say in the matter. I must remain silent,
submissive and full of gratitude, instead of being self-opinionated
and demanding. I found it all very difficult, and my on-going battle
with Edna and some of her colleagues greatly contributed to the
disillusionment and unhappiness I sometimes felt during my six
years at the school.

16

In the Care of Others

After two years, I joined a new class with a different attendant. The school was divided into junior and secondary sections, but because I was too young to become a secondary pupil, I was kept down a year to stay with my own age group. Although I was ahead of my classmates academically, I had so many physical difficulties in putting my work on paper that life became one long frustration. When I asked for more challenging work, the teacher said: 'You haven't even finished what you already have. How can you expect to get more?'

I needed constant physical help but I found it hard to attract attention. The teacher and attendant were often in deep conversation and I was unable to put my hand up because my muscles refused to work. If I resorted to asking for help, no one heard me and if I got so frustrated that I shouted out, I was told to shut up. As far as I was concerned my constant demands were the result of a deep desire to achieve. However, to most of my teachers they were thoroughly irritating.

I sat at my own desk in the corner, with my electric typewriter supported on a sloping wooden wedge. The attendant would plug in the machine, feed in the paper, open my book at the right page and place it on the reading stand in such a way that I could still see the teacher. My wheelchair had to be adjusted so that my hands could be placed in the correct position for typing. I could just hold my left wrist with my right hand and move it slowly around the keyboard so that my left index finger hit the keys. Sometimes it took three lessons to type out one page so I began cutting corners to get my work finished more quickly, which naturally affected the quality. In the end, I became so tired of the endless frustration that I took to trying to catch the teacher out. I would challenge her when she contradicted herself or remember quotations, gleaned from Nick, more accurately than she did. It irritated her like mad.

Once or twice she smacked a child who was indulging in a massive
tantrum, and I would fantasize about what I'd do if she ever tried
that with me.

My classmates were no consolation. They seemed so childish,
with their passion for Lego, puzzles and Ladybird books. I longed
to have sensible conversations but my overtures were usually
met with either a lack of comprehension or giggles. I was reading
Edgar Allen Poe at the time, and was particularly impressed by
one of his stories about someone being walled up. How I should
have loved to do that to one or two people I knew!

It was a tremendous relief when, at the age of twelve, I joined
the secondary school. Once again I mixed with older children, and
had a sense of stimulation and competition. Unfortunately, my
reputation for cheekiness had gone before me. Mrs Clark, my new
teacher, was all ready to crush any of my attempts to make a joke,
although my classmates could get away with it. But at least she
was consistent, with high expectations of her pupils. Her lessons
were always interesting and we were given homework for the first
time. We were allowed to be more independent and to make our
own rules after democratic discussion. And I was allowed to finish
my work during the breaks.

There was only one fly in the ointment – Edna was now my
class attendant again. Her antagonism towards me was as strong
as ever and thoroughly deflating. I lived in increasing dread of the
pain and ridicule which formed an integral part of the transfer into
my electric wheelchair each morning.

I got on with my classmates superficially, but really we had
nothing in common. I suppose my only proper school friend was
Nicky. About four years older than me, he suffered from a brittle
bone disease and had problems with his hearing. His parents
arranged for him to have extra lessons with his teacher, Mr
Sullivan, who sometimes played chess with me in the lunch hour. I
felt that at last I could talk to someone at my own level – although
I was rather at sea with most of our conversations which centred
around Nicky's problematic love life or lack of it!

Once our friendship was established, the headteacher asked
me to help Nicky with his oral examination in Communications.
This entailed attending some GCSE classes in which we acted or

debated. I enjoyed the debates so much, and did so well in them, that I shelved all other career plans and decided I would have to become a barrister.

Nicky passed all his exams. Since leaving school he has had a job in the local council office where he did his work experience. Although now stone deaf, he is a proficient lip-reader. His parents wheel him down to see me about once a week. The subject of our conversations hasn't changed much!

Steve was a different sort of friend from Nicky. Everyone liked his friendly, calm manner, as well as his eagerness to help anyone who was worse off than himself. He had been a perfectly healthy boy until, one day at primary school, his habit of rocking his chair backwards ended in disaster. He leant back too far, lost his balance and crashed into the wall behind, damaging his skull. This injury brought on epilepsy, which in turn caused a stroke with serious after-effects.

By now, my muscles had weakened so much that I found it difficult to operate my electric wheelchair. In some ways, this was a blessing because it meant I no longer had to submit to the early-morning transfer process with Edna. Instead, Steve became the perfect minder, happily pushing me around whenever I asked. Later on, he looked after me on our weekly trips for science lessons to a local college. Here we joined a class of children with emotional and behavioural difficulties. It was not an easy or natural mix. Most of us were quite delicate physically, but some of our new classmates could be unpredictable and violent. They also showed little interest in science, which was distracting for those of us who wanted to learn. This meant that we had been entered for the GCSEs at the lowest level. When it came to carrying out experiments, Olly and I made a great team. I gave the orders and he carried them out! I became the star pupil because I had already covered much of our school science work. I found it boring going over all this old ground, although I enjoyed it when the teacher sat on his own with me to take dictation and to answer my numerous questions.

Sadly, we were given a different teacher the following year. There were no more private sessions and I soon lost interest in science. I tried electronics but found it impossible even to begin the

process of building a radio. I couldn't hold anything properly –
least of all a soldering iron. I attempted desk-top publishing, but
found it just as hopeless. Because most of the pupils had learning
difficulties, the standard was low, and there was no one to help me
with my physical handicap. It seemed to me that nothing much
could be achieved by lumping together pupils with such diverse
problems.

Once I was in the secondary school, my social life picked up. I
had heard my classmates speak of St Mary's Club for disabled
teenagers, and one day Colin, its leader, turned up on our doorstep.
I happily accepted his offer of membership. Each week I was
collected by a local authority bus and taken to the meetings, which
I thoroughly enjoyed. Although I could not join in the table-top
games, at least I could watch. I let off steam playing wheelchair
football, which almost always ended up as a form of dodgem cars.

There was a friendly and relaxed atmosphere at the club.
Everyone helped each other and the staff were patient and kind.
Colin was universally liked. He had an empathy with each of us. He
was never patronizing, and joined in our activities as though there
were nothing in the world he would rather do. I cannot remember
him ever raising his voice – not that he had to, we were allowed so
much freedom. Colin understood perfectly our need to escape from
a never-ending dependence on others. In the environment which we
had created, our disabilities were forgotten and each one of us was
an individual.

Sadly, things were quite different when charities were involved.
Although grateful for the good intentions of people who want to
improve the lot of the disabled, I find it difficult to accept being
lumped together in a kind of crippled brotherhood in which all the
members are assumed to love each other's company and to revel in
the same activities whatever their ages, abilities or specific needs.

When I was twelve years old, the school received an invitation
to send a group of us to a Charity party which was to be held in a
famous hotel. We were reminded repeatedly how lucky we were to
be given such a treat in such a grand setting. As I sat in the school
bus on our way to the centre of London, I looked forward eagerly to
being wheeled into the impressive entrance of the hotel in which I
was going to be treated like the film stars and important people

who stayed there. A bowing flunky would push me through a huge, ornate hall decked with dripping chandeliers on our way to the magnificent dining room with its glamorous waitresses who were to attend to my every whim.

How different was the reality! On arrival I found myself shivering on the pavement waiting for my turn to be pushed across the road to join the others. The next thing we knew was that our wheelchairs were being seized by various people and pushed rapidly round the corner into a dingy alleyway towards a kind of gate. I realised with a stab of disappointment that, instead of making a grand entrance, I was to enter the hotel in the service lift. A group of sullen-looking young men manhandled my wheelchair into it without saying a word and we went down to land with a bump. As the gates were pulled back, I saw to my horror that we were still about three feet off the floor. Someone positioned a rough wooden plank to act as a frighteningly steep ramp and I was told to go. I closed my eyes, activated my wheelchair and hurtled downwards!

All the pupils from my school sat at the same table. The first thing we noticed, with some consternation, was the cutlery. It was plastic. For normal people this would present no problem, but for the disabled or clumsy it was a different matter. A boy with cerebral palsy looked around and announced 'Oh well, I'll be having plastic for my tea!' We all knew that he could have a spasm while eating which would result in a mouthful of broken cutlery. The pliable plastic cups also presented a problem. If he gripped too hard there would be liquid flying in all directions. The only solution was for someone to feed him.

The entertainment began with two comedians. Whilst I was able to appreciate the humour, their act went over the heads of the younger members of the audience who could only respond to something more visual. However, they were thrilled when several famous footballers appeared dressed in their strip. Watching the ensuing scene from the sidelines, I couldn't help feeling sorry for both the celebrities and the children. The footballers looked like fish out of water as they stood with arms folded and fixed smiles of embarrassment on their faces as eager young fans surged towards them, some on crutches, wheelchairs, or walking frames, others crawling or lurching along on callipers. Chocolate-covered faces grinned and dribbled with excitement as their heroes' expressions showed only too clearly how unused they were to meeting such children. I felt sad about their discomfort. And rather angry about my own when I asked one of the school attendants to take me to the toilet. There was no cubicle big enough to accommodate a wheelchair, so I was presented with a 'bottle' in the middle of the washroom and required to 'Get a move on' by the attendant who had no intention of missing any more of the entertainment. I struggled to fill the bottle under the gaze of the continuous stream of people making for the toilets. My humiliation was complete when I found myself unable to perform!

Fortunately, the disco had begun and I joined in the fun although I could not help feeling a familiar twinge of frustration at being segregated from the able-bodied. I reflected that, if social events for the young included all sections of society, they would learn to accept each other whilst still free from prejudice and before the inevitable barriers are put up. As we jigged around in our wheelchairs or shuffled about on zimmer frames, the lights went up and we were summoned to the front of the hall to receive rather smart looking blue holdalls. I was delighted with my present until I caught sight of the huge white letters printed on one side – 'The — Charity's Christmas Party for Underprivileged Children'. I burned with resentment. However disabled I may be I was NOT underprivileged. Anyway, I couldn't bring myself to use the bag which so blatantly advertised the generosity of a charity towards such a pitiable creature as myself.

I drove myself furiously towards the long, steep staircase in front of which we had been told to assemble. Apparently it was not possible to get us into the service lifts so groups of four soldiers hoisted a wheelchair onto their shoulders and set off up the stairs. I closed my eyes as the ever-present terror of being tipped out of my chair rendered me speechless. Once back in the safety of the school bus, I thought over the events of the afternoon and wondered if I should try to be more grateful to those who meant well even though their often patronising attitude seemed so intolerable at times.

17

The View from a Hospital Bed

Throughout this period, I attended King's College Hospital regularly. Since the pneumonia episode, I had become dependent on antibiotics and was now a patient of Professor Price. One day I was given an appointment to see another of my consultants, Mr Morley, at the Royal National Orthopaedic Hospital (RNOH) in Stanmore. Although I had been wearing a body brace made by the technicians at King's, Mr Morley told me that my spine was becoming so crooked that it would eventually crush my lungs and kill me. I needed an operation to prevent this curvature from becoming worse.

In due course I was admitted to the huge children's ward at the RNOH, little realizing that it was be my home for the next four months. Just as I was building up my courage to go through with the operation, Mr Morley came to see me. He looked very serious. 'I'm afraid we can't go ahead,' he said. 'You see, the tests have shown that your lungs are too weak to withstand the amount of anaesthetic which you'd need for the operation.'

I felt thoroughly deflated. What was to become of me? Mr Morley continued. 'There *is* an alternative treatment. It's called 'halo traction' and means that we would fit a sort of iron ring round your head, held on by four bolts driven into your skull. We will attach a pulley with weights on it to the halo, and that will help to stretch out your spine. If that is successful, it may just be possible to perform the operation.'

I listened in horror. It all sounded like something out of *Frankenstein*. But I soon realized that I had no choice, and agreed to undergo the treatment. So began one of the hardest periods of my life. I think I could go through almost anything else again, but not that.

The first step was to give me a mild anaesthetic while the bolts were screwed into my head. Although terrified by the whole business, I had now convinced myself that it would make my lungs better. I had seen other children in the ward going through a bad time before they got well again, and I wanted to be one of them.

I woke up in intensive care, feeling drowsy and light-headed. My voice sounded echoey and distant. An hour later, I would have happily welcomed death. I had developed the worst headache it is possible to imagine, made worse by the knowledge that what I was feeling was actually true – there really *were* four bolts screwed into my skull.

Mum stood outside the ward, paralysed by my screams. Eventually, I tried to roll over to sleep but was stopped by a screw sticking two miles out of my forehead. I felt like a freak. For the next two days I vomited up everything. My head felt like a lead ball and I cried for Mum between drug-induced bouts of sleep. In spite of her brave face I knew she was suffering at the sight of me in such a state.

Gradually, I began to feel a little more normal. I was able to eat and use a bedpan – a public and embarrassing procedure. It was a relief to return to the children's ward. Soon doctors and technicians arrived to fit a new contraption to my bed and wheelchair. A nylon cord ran from my halo through a pulley and over the head of the bed. Attached to it was a series of plates, each weighing 1 pound. One of these was to be attached each day until my spine was being stretched by a weight of 16 kilos.

The bed was tilted up at an angle of 45 degrees to enable me to sleep. All that prevented me from falling out was the weights holding me back by my head. To my amazement, I could now lie on my side, despite the bolts sticking into my pillow – It was just as well, because sleeping on my back is dangerous in case I swallow my saliva and choke.

My first attempt at sitting in a chair was miserably uncomfortable. At this stage, the halo seemed to weigh a ton and I felt crushed by it. However as another weight was added each day, I found I could lift my head more easily and sit for longer periods at a time. The curvature was improving and I no longer needed to wear the brace, which was a big boost to my morale.

Mum says I looked almost normal, except for the contraption on my head! All the nurses were kind. One of them, Sarah, brought me a video to watch each day which helped me to make friends with the other kids as they gathered around to watch with me. I also persuaded the Sister to let us stay up until midnight at weekends. However, there was no changing bedtimes when there were any really sick children on the ward.

Once I was stable and my treatment became routine, I put all thoughts of it out of my head and concentrated on day-to-day living. The teachers arrived at 8 o'clock each morning and helped the nurses to get us ready for lessons. English was my best subject, so I soon struck up a relationship with the English teacher, Mr Davies. He reminded me of Nick. Although quiet on the surface, both men had a great sense of humour.

Mr Davies taught me such a lot. It was through him that I learnt about atoms. I didn't write down much of what he said, but I remember how interesting our conversations were – sometimes they lasted for three hours or more.

Design and technology lessons were also fun. I had often imagined designing cities, cars, machines and, especially, underground bunkers to be used in the event of a nuclear explosion. I needed to ensure my survival. My teacher helped me to design what I was firmly convinced were works of genius. Best of all was a wonderful writing box full of compartments and secret drawers. It never actually got built, but the design was superb!

Other teachers taught cooking, history, geography, maths, Spanish, French and crafts. I even tried to learn to type properly but ended up using my old prodding method. Computers made things easier and each pupil was fixed up with suitable equipment. I enjoyed the busy atmosphere and all the attention I received from the staff of the hospital school.

The ward itself felt like home in a way. I belonged to an extended family and was spoilt by the nurses who, whenever I could persuade them, took me for walks in the nearby woods. The domestic assistant, who spoke Spanish, would let me sleep late in the mornings and even kept my breakfast warm for me until I woke up.

Many of my fellow patients suffered from conditions which

made me feel quite lucky by comparison. In fact, they gave me courage. I especially remember Theo, a twelve-year-old boy from Corsica. When I first met him, his leg was so swollen that I thought it would burst. At that time I had a persistent chest infection which meant I often woke up coughing at night, I would lie there and listen to Theo screaming with pain. Both with strong, rather competitive personalities, we were not really friends, but his unhappiness always affected me.

Osmond, a Turkish Cypriot, reminded me of Sinbad the Sailor. He felt antagonistic towards Theo and boasted proudly that, were they not in hospital, they would be sworn enemies. He was rather large and fierce-looking, all that was missing were baggy trousers, pointed shoes and a scimitar! In his locker he kept a hoard of food which he guarded jealously, but at the same time he apparently felt entitled to help himself to mine! I couldn't afford to complain. He was bigger than me and not bright enough to conduct a reasonable argument – my only form of defence. I realise now that Osmond's aggression was triggered by pain and fear. His description of phantom pains in his amputated legs never ceased to fascinate me.

The doctor's had to amputate Theo's leg and for a time he seemed to improve, even playing snooker in his wheelchair. But suddenly he was moved to a small side room. The nurses said it was so he would not keep us awake at night, but we soon guessed that it was to spare us from seeing his suffering. One day I sat watching TV as usual with my friend Randolph, whose bed was next to Theo's room. Suddenly, Theo's mum ran out of the side room, in floods of tears. Randolph and I looked at each other in silence. We knew that Theo was dead. I felt mortal and very vulnerable.

One Sunday afternoon, half-way through my stay at the RNOH, Colin arrived at my bedside. He had noticed my absence at several club evenings and decided to track me down. So began another friendship which is still going strong. Colin, a carpenter by trade, soon discovered my penchant for designing intricate and amazingly useful boxes. We spent many afternoons deep in satisfying discussions about my inventions and their feasibility. Colin's evident interest in even my most far-fetched schemes provided a boost to my already healthy ego!

From early childhood, I have been fascinated by weapons. Knowing that I could rely on Colin's help, I began to design swords and knives. Once I had left the hospital, Colin appeared on our doorstep (every Saturday afternoon) with his bag of tools. We would sit in the garage while I issued instructions and he worked on pieces of wood. I revelled in watching my ideas being brought to life. Unfortunately most of my fearsome Samurai swords met an early end due to my compulsion to get someone to test their breaking point. Undaunted by my destructive instincts, Colin quietly carried on translating my ideas into reality. At the same time, we discussed everything from women to Colin's particular interest, the two World Wars.

Over the years he has played an increasingly important part in my life, providing steady friendship and practical help. Always reliable and generous with his time, I know I can ask him to drive me and my wheelchair to a war museum, weapons shop or hospital appointment. Although I have outgrown my inventive phase, we still spend long hours each week deep in conversation.

After I had spent more than three months attached to the halo, my surgeon sent me to the Brompton Hospital in London, which specializes in diseases of the chest, to find out if my lungs could now cope with a large dose of general anaesthetic. Having set out with high hopes, I was devastated to be told that all the stretching from the halo traction had not improved my breathing sufficiently. I returned to the RNOH in despair.

The next day was a Tuesday – the day for my surgeon's weekly visit. It was always a worry in case he gave me bad news, but now I was so nervous that, as Mr Morley appeared in the doorway, I was violently sick. He asked to speak to Mum privately. It seemed to me that they were closeted together for ages, and my heart sank when I eventually saw Mum's anguished face. I demanded to know the reason for her sadness but she seemed tongue-tied and reluctant to speak.

'You aren't responsible for my life!' I shouted. 'I have the right to know what you've been told.' Then despair got the better of me. 'Why the hell was I ever born?' That was the only time I've ever felt so negative. What I really want is to live long enough for the doctors to find a cure for muscular atrophy. In the meantime I have no desire to be told how long I've got. It is better to enjoy each day than to dwell on how many (or how few) I have left.

Close to tears, Mum told me what Mr Morley had said. Apparently, he felt that a successful operation on my spine might prolong my life, but it would be a huge gamble. The poor state of my lungs could kill me and, at the very best, I would be on a life-support machine for some time after the operation. If I then contracted one of my routine chest infections, it would be fatal. My body would not be able to support the intensive physiotherapy needed to remove the mucus from my lungs. Mr Morley had told Mum: 'The choice is yours.'

She looked at me sadly, then said: 'I've decided you're not going to go through with it. You can't.' I insisted on seeing Mr Morley myself, but he confirmed my worst fears. Although he could operate, there was no guarantee that I would survive the operation, yet without it my life expectancy would be shorter. 'I'll give you two weeks to decide,' he told me.

At first I felt as though I had been given a reprieve, but as time went on I began frantically asking everyone for their opinion. Friends, teachers, nurses were all kind, and all remained neutral.

Each day I reversed my decision. Although outwardly unchanged, I struggled to fend off panic and depression.

At the end of the first week it was time to remove the halo. To my horror I recognized the technician, a junior doctor whom I had grown to hate. He was the one who had visited me every two days to tighten the screws in my skull. Totally impassive, he could have been the plumber fixing a tap! He met my attempts at conversation with a few abrupt words or nothing at all. On one horrible day he came to take blood. Unable to find a vein, he kept jabbing the needle back into my arm, waggling it around hopefully. By the third attempt I gave up my pretence at bravery. My screams must have thoroughly unnerved the man. Suddenly he pulled out the needle, threw it across the floor and stalked out of the ward!

Now we were face to face again. I had expected to be given some sort of anaesthetic but could see no sign of one. Instead, my old adversary was armed with a screwdriver. I prepared myself for the worst but, to my surprise, I felt nothing apart from the violent twisting of my head. Apparently, there are no nerves in the skull.

What was awful was hearing in my head the echo of screw grating against bone, then feeling the pain when the skin near the screw holes became twisted around the screwdriver. I suppose we were as relieved as each other when it was all over.

Paradoxically, the removal of the heavy halo and its weights caused my head to feel as though it weighed a ton. It instantly flopped down on to my chest, which was humiliating and frustrating. Once again, I was reminded of my helplessness. I also missed the benefits of the halo – it may have looked frightening, but it had meant that I could sit up straight and tall without having to wear my hated brace. My stretched-out spine had dramatically improved my breathing and, as a consequence, my sense of well-being. Now I realised sadly that I was back to square one and as weird and ugly as ever. I had always tried to convince myself that, although I might not look like a film star, it could be much worse. Now that no longer seemed to be true. I was deformed. The months I had spent in hospital felt like a waste of time and I burst into tears. Mum tried to comfort me but was soon in tears herself. Later, I was given a neck-support to relieve the ache of trying to hold up my head. The doctors reassured me that eventually I would be able to manage it on my own once more.

The days passed quickly, and soon it was the Tuesday when I had to tell Mr Morley my decision. I felt thoroughly sick as I watched him walk up the ward. Even now I was still unsure what I would say. My Morley approached my bed, greeted me and looked expectant. Suddenly, I found myself speaking. 'I've decided not to go through with it.' Mr Morley let out a loud sigh of relief and almost congratulated me. He had clearly dreaded the thought of attempting what would have been a dangerous and difficult operation. I too felt thankful at having finally reached a decision, and also quite philosophical. After all, I was very much alive and intended to stay that way.

One evening, not long before I was due to leave hospital, I was waiting for supper when I looked up and saw Aunt Teresa's boyfriend standing by my bed. My hackles rose immediately, and I felt Mum stiffen.

'Hello,' he said. 'Diego's grandmother and aunts are waiting outside.'

'Oh, really?' Mum replied in a cool voice. Her unspoken 'So what?' hung in the air.

I looked nervously towards the ward doors and saw Teresa's small daughter peering through at me. All the old resentment and anger welled up and my imagination ran riot as I pictured them all coming back when Mum was not around to protect me. Teresa's boyfriend hesitated, then reluctantly turned and left. I watched tensely as they all walked away.

A few days later, I received a get-well card from Grandmother. Mum looked at it and said she had been thinking things over. Perhaps we should try to build a few bridges. After all, we could not really afford to turn away support from our only relatives in London. Mum finally persuaded me to ring Grandmother. Our conversation was stilted and trivial, but it marked the turning point in our relationship. At last she saw me as an equal and not a dependent child. Over the years we have built up a working relationship. The past is never mentioned even though Mum now spends long periods on the phone each week chatting to her mother in law.

I have forgiven Grandmother for her apparently cruel treatment. Perhaps she thought she was acting in my best interests. But Luz is another matter. She remains the focus of all my anger about my first year in England.

At last, it was time to leave hospital. I could almost support the weight of my head again, and I was fitted with a new plastic body brace, which had been made from a plaster of Paris mould of my body during the time it was being stretched out by the halo. I felt a mixture of emotions: huge disappointment at the time wasted on what had proved to be a hopeless enterprise, but also gratitude for the efforts that had been made on my behalf by the doctors and nurses and also for the education and attention I had received from the teachers. It had all been quite informal but I had learned a lot and that gave me confidence. There had been much fun and laughter, but also immense sadness in seeing the pain and stress experienced by my fellow patients and their families. I was glad to be leaving that behind, as well as the memories of my own discomfort and disappointment.

There was another reason why I could not wait to go home.

Orlando, my little brother, was arriving in England the following day. He had spent the past three years living with Eduardo, his girlfriend and their new baby daughter. According to some of the workers in Eduardo's factory, his girlfriend had felt she had to compete with Orlando for his father's attention, and that had made life difficult all round. It must have been with some relief that Eduardo agreed to let Orlando spend his summer holidays with us.

Two of Eduardo's female relatives, who lived in Essex, drove us to the airport that morning. We had made contact and grown very close to them while we were living with Albel's family in south London. We set off, full of excitement, and soon stood impatiently behind the rails in the arrivals lounge. The plane was late and Mum became so agitated that she had to keep dashing off to the ladies' room. Eventually, she went off to find the information desk. Just as she disappeared I saw a small, grinning figure sitting on top of a pile of luggage which was being pushed along by a stewardess. Orlando leaped off the trolley and rushed towards us. Mum returned to find us hugging and kissing as though our lives depended on it!

It was wonderful to be reunited with Orlando. He was bright, funny and confident. It seemed as if we had never been parted. I felt proud, protective and eager to teach him all I knew. Very soon he assumed responsibility for as many of my physical needs as he could manage. He showed absolutely no resentment at having to look after me – partly because of his placid and generous nature and partly because of the family expectation that each member would help another without question. For the first time I had the feeling that I was truly the head of our household.

Orlando did not return to Colombia at the end of the summer holidays. Eduardo's sister, Joanna, had recently arrived in England from Colombia and she dropped so many sinister hints about the goings-on in Eduardo's household that Mum was convinced it was no longer the right place for Orlando to live. She rang Eduardo to tell him and he tearfully accepted the situation. Then she found a school for Orlando, a bus-ride away from our flat. Because Mum could not leave me by myself, Orlando had to get himself to and from school without knowing a word of English.

Mum's contentment at having both her sons with her once again was increased because she now had more time to herself. Confident that Orlando would look after me, she enjoyed herself window-shopping or seeing friends. She lost the strained look she had worn for so long as our lives settled into a fairly predictable pattern, broken only by my periodic chest infections or the dramas that Mum and her friends managed to conjure up!

18

Puberty Strikes!

When I was thirteen, puberty hit me with a vengeance. Suddenly, my dependence on others assumed massive proportions. All my life I had needed help to use the toilet or a bottle, and I had never thought twice about the intimacy it entailed. But, without warning, 'things' started to happen to me. The only part of my body to function completely normally stood up with alarming enthusiasm! I found myself suddenly embarrassed and unable to do anything in front of the attendants, especially the more attractive ones! I would frantically try to clear my mind, repeating over and over to myself, 'It will not happen today' – to no avail. Even the thought of one of those women unzipping my trousers was enough to set things off. To be honest, there were times when I wondered what *would* happen if I lost control – probably an instant death from shame! On the other hand, part of me half-wanted something to happen. Otherwise how would I ever know what it felt like? I began to avoid asking the younger attendants to toilet me. That worked most of the time, but even when an older, unattractive woman was doing the necessary, I never quite knew if my natural instincts would get the better of me.

Sex was always on my mind. I found it impossible to rid myself of its constant demands. For several years, every girl I saw represented a kind of torture. Now, at the ripe old age of twenty, I am no longer beset by such frequent and violent urges. I have learned to control and sublimate them to some extent, although I sometimes feel deeply sad at the possibility of never experiencing a sex life. I sometimes get the impression that many of the able-bodied imagine that the disabled are not interested in sex. Wrong! But I am convinced that there are people in my position whose emotional state is affected by the frustration of their predicament, not only because of their physical urges but because they want to join the rest of the human race in experiencing what is, after all, only natural.

My Latin American heritage does nothing to help the situation. As I come from a society which so applauds overtly virile men that a faithful husband is almost someone to be despised, it sometimes feels as though the Colombian part of me is continually under threat from my inability to prove my sexuality.

Eduardo's example is another big influence. As soon as I became aware of it, I admired his prodigious ability to attract and ensnare good-looking women. After sufficient probing from me and Mum, Orlando admitted that he often accompanied his father on assignations. Apparently, Eduardo would manufacture an argument with his live-in girlfriend so that he could then walk out in disgust and sometimes not return for days at time. It seemed that nothing had changed!

19

Colombia: Returning Home

Two years passed. Eduardo, who was now living in New York, regularly sent Mum money for Orlando's keep. His generosity meant that life became easier for all three of us as well as enabling Mum to save for an emergency or a holiday. After many lengthy discussions, Mum and I decided to visit Colombia. We missed our family and the way of life, with its warmth and gaiety. By now I was mixing memories with fantasy, so in my imagination the country was positively Utopian.

We planned our journey carefully. My two doctors agreed to let me travel on the condition that I left England in the peak of health and armed with antibiotics and an oxygen cylinder, in case I had problems during the flight. We made all the medical arrangements, and Professor Price, my chest specialist, wrote to the airline to persuade them to take the risk of flying me. Eduardo paid for Orlando's ticket and Mum used some of her savings to pay for herself and me.

I had just begun my GCSE course at school, but the teachers agreed that I could repeat the year when I returned. Colin and I hastily put the finishing touches to our latest invention – a portable wooden commode. The idea had been to construct a collapsible light-weight waterproof wooden contraption, complete with back and arm supports. This could then be used under a shower or wheeled over any lavatory seat I might encounter. Our impressive feat of design and engineering fulfilled all the criteria except one. Although it's components fitted neatly into a suitcase, they might as well have been made of lead. It was poor Orlando's misfortune to have the job of carting around this vital piece of luggage.

When the great day arrived, Colin drove us all to the airport. I was determined not to show how emotional I felt, but it was difficult. I was going home, and thought: 'This must be how pilgrims feel when they are on their way to Mecca.'

Most of our fellow travellers were Colombians. Some were going on holiday but others were obviously being deported. Their differing states of mind contributed to a peculiar atmosphere. Gazing around, I saw some passengers' faces wreathed in smiles, whilst others looked so distraught that I almost expected them to jump out of a window. One man was taking huge gulps from a bottle of whisky which he imagined to be camouflaged by a paper bag. His misery was complete when the stewardess relieved him of his medicine before he could complete the required dose.

The flight was rather an ordeal for the three of us. My long-suffering mother and brother had to endure hours of discomfort while I lay across them in my stiff brace. But at least my breathing was normal and I had no need of the oxygen. One man took it upon himself to act as our guardian – more out of interest in Mum than sympathy for my plight, I suspect.

To my astonishment, a huge cheer went up as we landed at Bogotá airport. I felt like joining in. Images flashed across my mind – serried ranks of relatives waiting with outstretched arms, friendly chatty people in such places as hospital waiting rooms or bus queues, parties, music, gossip and, best of all, girls. My cousins must have a lot of friends by now and the doorstep culture would give me a chance to win some over with my superior intellect and charm. 'Please God, let me find a girlfriend,' I prayed. 'Let me prove that, even with my handicap, I am a genuine red-blooded Colombian male.'

I was lifted up by our new-found friend and, as we started down the steps, I caught sight of Aunt Esneda's son, Jairo. Now a police officer in Palmira, he had been allowed through the strict airport security by his colleagues in Bogotá. Policemen in Colombia live under permanent threat of death from criminals. Their necessary dependence on one another forms close bonds. The last time I had seen Jairo, he had cried as he waved goodbye to a small boy on his way to England. Now I laughed when I saw the look on this face as he recognized me and heard my newly-deepened 14 year old-voice. During the hectic period which followed, I realized for the first time that I had been wearing rose-coloured spectacles when I thought about Colombia. In England, life was so much easier for the disabled. After Mum and Jairo had made a huge fuss, I finally ended up in an enormous, ancient wheelchair in which I slithered and bounced my way towards the chaotic airport terminal. We had to take an internal flight to Cali, but one look at the crowded minibus provided for the journey to the smaller airport and Mum became distraught.

'I can't take him in there. It's quite impossible. You'll have to provide something else,' she yelled. Twenty minutes later, an elderly truck appeared and we all struggled up on to the high front seat. Battered and bruised, we tore into the small scruffy airport building, only to discover that we had missed our connection and must now sit, sweltering and furious, for four hours until the next flight. But our frustration and weariness vanished when we touched down in Cali. A huge reception party awaited us. Before I had a chance to take it all in, I was being clutched to bosom after ample bosom. Coming up for air, I caught sight of the glamorous young women who had been my little cousins. I fervently wished that it was they who were giving me such a rapturous welcome!

We piled into someone's car for the last stage of the journey. As we drove towards Palmira I felt my skin shrivelling up in the unaccustomed heat. I looked out at the miles and miles of sugar cane, the monotony of the landscape broken only by the huge, garish advertisement hoardings which screamed their wares as we shot past along the wide motorway. I felt quite light-headed with joy when I recognized the outskirts of Palmira. Another reception committee was waiting on the pavement outside Aunt Esnedá's house, where we were to stay. I felt a pang when I remembered she would not be there. Everyone gasped at the change in me and I revelled in playing the returning celebrity, although I felt decidedly put out when my cousins Tania and Gloria barely acknowledged me. I could hardly keep my eyes off them, but told myself optimistically that, although *they* may be off-limits, their friends certainly would not be.

20

Girls, Girls, Girls

As the days passed, I met more and more girls. Gloria would come home from school and take me out, but to my disappointment her friends seemed to regard me as a little brother rather than a potential boyfriend. Sometimes I took Gloria out to a restaurant or to the cinema, using money that had been given to me by friends and relatives in England. For the first time, I was able to act out my fantasy of being the Great Gatsby. How I had envied his life and success with women when we read the book in class. Now I was thrilled when I seemed to be able to attract girls without much trouble. It didn't occur to me that my novelty value, apparent wealth and ability to speak English contributed to my success quite as much as my natural charm!

Orlando went to stay with Eduardo's mother, and his father flew over from New York to be with them. His girlfriend stayed behind, which was probably just as well as it was considered part of Orlando's education to watch his father in action. However, I was the one who really appreciated Eduardo's skills in the art of flirtation. I loved to watch how he cast a spell over his victims. *He* really *was* the Great Gatsby.

Mum and I settled into our own routine. She took over the running of the house and such furious cleaning, shopping and cooking went on for Gloria, Jairo and their father that I had to wait until 11 o'clock each morning before Mum had time to begin the long process of getting me up. She and I slept on the ground floor so that I could use the toilet which had been installed for Aunt Esneda once she became too ill to climb the stairs. Mum undressed me, lifted me on to Colin's commode and wheeled me over the toilet seat. Next came the business of washing which took place in the corridor which housed a sink and drainage hole in the floor. Mum attached a hose to the tap and sprayed me as I sat on my throne full of fear that Gloria might come down the stairs to see me in all my highly-questionable glory!

Mum spent many afternoons gossiping with neighbours and renewing old friendships. I enjoyed seeing her so animated and happy now that she was back in her own environment. Each evening, everyone sat outside, either on their front steps or in the local park. If Gloria was not around, one of her friends would push me to the corner of the street where there was always a gathering around Franzeddy, the local lottery ticket seller, who became my firm friend as we watched the world go by. Sometimes we left Palmira to visit Mum's home town of Toro. For me it was filled with memories of childhood and happy times spent with my great-grandmother and her daughters, but, in reality, it is one of the most dangerous places in Colombia being situated in a valley surrounded by mountains covered in cocaine plantations. It was not unusual for people setting off for work in the early morning to see dead bodies lying in the street, the victims of Colombia's thriving drug trade. The army and police take little notice, and the town's inhabitants turn a blind eye. There is no point in inviting one's own execution by helping the authorities.

One evening, Mum, Orlando and I were taking part in the doorstep ritual when we heard a group of girls calling our names. They must have recognized me from early childhood. After plucking up courage, I persuaded Orlando to wheel me over to them. I found one girl called Martha particularly attractive. She must have been about nineteen and told me that she had left her boyfriend because he would not take her seriously. I pricked up my ears. Maybe this was my chance.

When Martha questioned me about my love-life, I launched into a completely fictitious sob-story about my ex-girlfriend who had heartlessly abandoned me for my best friend because she had got tired of being with a boy in a wheelchair. I piled on the agony so much that I started to feel really sorry for myself.

That night, I lay awake wondering how I could ensnare Martha. What would my hero Eduardo do, I wondered. I decided to buy her a present. After all, it was Christmas week. The following day, I persuaded a friend to take me shopping. We bought a sentimental record called *Martha*. Perfect! But when Mum discovered it she persuaded me to put it away. I think she was trying to prevent me from making a fool of myself.

On New Year's Eve we all joined Martha's family for the traditional street party. The 'Old Year' was sitting on top of a car, waiting to be shown off to the neighbours. It was a bit like the 'Guy' which British people burn on Bonfire Night, and was filled with fireworks. At midnight it would be set on fire and all the badness of the old year would go up in flames. I looked at the effigy lolling sideways on the car roof, and remembered that Aunt Esneda's nickname for me had been 'Old Year', because of my floppiness and inability to sit up unaided.

When I saw that Mum and the rest of the family were safely out of earshot, I managed to get myself alone with Martha in her front room. I gave her my present, and was delighted when she refused to go out with her friends who called round. We talked about my fake life, which I liberally embellished with stories about my wealth and brilliance, and Martha's unhappiness because her family insisted that it was time she got married. I told her that if I married a foreign girl I could take her to Britain on my passport – quite untrue, of course, and I was all of 14 years old! Convinced that Martha was interested, I asked her to be my girlfriend. She looked at me with horror and muttered: 'I'll have to think about it.' There was nothing more to say, so I asked her to take me outside again. She went off to another party, leaving me feeling foolish and abandoned. At midnight, the fire station let off a siren which shrieked out its welcome to the new year. That was the signal for a frantic round of hugging, kissing and crying. People crowded round me. Suddenly, through the throng, I saw Martha. She bent over and kissed me on the mouth. I was astonished. My heart beat wildly and it felt as though all the blood was rushing to my head. I thought, 'My God, I'm going to get a nose bleed.' Not very romantic, but it had been so shocking, and she had used her tongue. What did it mean? Was she now my girlfriend? I had been so determined to prove my manhood that I had not bargained for feeling naïve and immature now that something had happened. To make matters worse, Mum voiced my hidden fears by telling me she was worried I was making a fool of myself, and that Martha was only interested in my money which was fast running out anyway.

Martha and I began a strange relationship, which I still can't understand. She spent so much time talking about her ex-boy friend that I wondered what she wanted with me. I was ashamed and frustrated that I now had to ask her to kiss me. Even that was something I could not do on my own. Sometimes I used to think: 'I may not be Tom Cruise, but why do I have to be Quasimodo?' One evening I asked Martha if she was a virgin. Despite her shock at my question, she replied 'No.' My male ego reacted with hurt and resentment.

Martha also seemed to be very choosy about who she introduced me to. Why wouldn't she let me meet her friends? I took her to a disco, but it was clear that she was bored just sitting at a table with me, and when a young man asked me if he could dance with her, I feigned indifference.

I became tired of my so-called girlfriend's moans about her misery at home, and how much she wanted to leave. Her parents could hardly bear the sight of me and ignored all my efforts to charm them into liking me. In my innocence, I thought that was a good sign. All my role-models had told me that their parents-in-law hated them. Surely, then, that meant I was getting something right? I quite fancied myself as the son-in-law from hell.

I was rather relieved when we returned to Palmira. Martha and I kept in touch by phone, but I became increasingly critical of her, perhaps to protect myself from the inevitable outcome. For all its, perhaps illusory, promise the relationship was the result of two people's very different needs.

Mum and Eduardo had decided that Orlando should take his first Communion in Colombia, with a big party afterwards. It seemed a very good idea, not least because it would all be paid for by Eduardo, who seemed to need to impress Mum with his generosity. Perhaps guilt also had something to do with it.

It was going to be a big do, and I decided to invite Martha. If she had been making fun of me, I was prepared to retaliate in my own way. I wanted desperately to show Eduardo that I had learned from his shining example as a Lothario. I got carried away by my thoughts, 'perhaps now I'll get the chance to get her into bed so that I can do my duty as a Colombian male'. But my half-baked plans looked even more pointless when Martha insisted that she

could not come without both her sisters, and that she needed a new
dress. Grandly I offered to pay for that and for the return cab fare
from Toro. Caught up in my own fantasy, I knew that I would have
to go through the Colombian courting ritual if I were to stand a
chance with her.

I waited eagerly for the girls to arrive, but when I saw Martha
again my heart sank. Somehow, her appeal had quite vanished.
What had I ever seen in her? She and her sisters were packed into
our over-crowded household, but they made no effort to help with
the frantic preparations. I began to wonder what I had done, and
spent most of my time trying to avoid them.

The great day arrived. Eduardo had taken over a whole restaurant, which was situated on an island in the middle of a lake. Cooks
and waiters dispensed lavish amounts of food and clowns had been
hired to entertain us. To my disgust, I was put in front of them.
As Martha and I sat watching their infantile antics, I thought
resentfully: 'Here I am struggling to get through the door of
manhood and all they do is drag me back.'

Eduardo kept appearing with a knowing look on his face, clearly
meant to indicate his approval of my status as part of a 'couple'. I
was not sure whether I was pleased or insulted by his broad winks.
He and Mum behaved as though nothing had really changed
between them, although that did not prevent him from flirting with
every other woman at the party. As soon as decently possible, I
abandoned Martha and sat at Eduardo's table so I could watch him
in action. The more he drank, the more he teased me, saying: 'Come
on, let's see you give Martha a kiss. We'll take a photo of the great
happening.' Martha was summoned, but when I refused to go
through with it, she ran off in tears. I felt silly and self-conscious
at being expected to perform for a half-drunk audience. I found
Martha and told her that our relationship was over. What a relief! I
felt free again. Besides, I told myself, there were plenty of other
girls about.

At midnight, the drinks licence ran out, so we all repaired to
Eduardo's house. I talked to everyone and watched him dancing
with Mum again. Within an hour, he was very drunk and sobbing
his heart out dramatically. Paradoxically, this is quite acceptable
behaviour for a Colombian man. Crying in public is definitely not

allowed unless drunkenness can be used as an excuse, in which case the floodgates open and there is a wonderfully self-indulgent wallowing in all the miseries of life.

A group of young people saw their chance and persuaded Eduardo to hand over the keys of his new sports car. One of his nephews took the wheel as we all piled in and set out on a wild joy-ride, tearing up and down the straight streets with the horn blaring. I absolutely loved it. At last I felt as though I were a normal teenager. Miraculously, we got back to the party in one piece, only to find that Eduardo's mother had announced that the party had finished.

I woke up late the following morning. No one seemed to be around except Martha, who had slept in the adjoining room. When I heard her moving about I called her in. The moment I saw her in her nightie, my frustrated need to prove myself resurfaced. 'I may not get another opportunity like this for a long time,' I told myself, as I motioned her to sit beside me on the bed. I rambled on about feeling that she did not really care for me unless she could prove it.

'How can I do that?' Martha asked.

'Make love to me,' I replied, quick as a flash. After a shocked silence she refused to even consider such an idea. I started to coax and reason with her, until it seemed she was prepared to lie down on the bed with me. I heard Mum's footsteps on the stairs. That was the nearest I have ever got to any kind of sexual relationship. I had failed in my duty to prove my manhood.

Martha left the following day. When I heard later that she had talked Eduardo into paying for her cab back to Toro, I felt ashamed and insulted. I had already paid her fare, as well she knew. Perhaps, after all, Martha had just seen me as a passport to England.

I put the whole thing down to experience and continued my quest. Looking back, I realize how presumptuous, vain and egocentric I was. At the age of fourteen, I expected to have girls falling at my feet. It had not even occurred to me that a nineteen-year-old girl like Martha was highly unlikely to be interested in me – even if I had been a perfect physical specimen. I still expected to command the attention I had received when I was a cute little boy trapped in a wheelchair, yet able to talk like an adult with astonishing confidence. Suddenly I faced competition where there had been none, I was becoming more 'ordinary', with the added disadvantage of my increasing disability. Children who had lagged behind me in their development had caught up and were now enjoying experiences which seemed to be out of my reach.

I resolved to try pastures new, but when I made a gauche approach to one of her friends, my cousin Gloria was so embarrassed that she no longer included me in her gang. Without anyone to push me I had no option but to move my hunting ground back to the lottery seller's pitch. Franzeddy, who had known me all my life, was about thirty. She was a small, slim, dark-skinned woman who, although reluctant to admit it, was an expert at drawing her customer's secrets out of them without them realizing it. The better she got to know her customers, the more tickets they bought from her.

One hot morning, when we were putting the world to rights as usual, I noticed a teenage girl approaching the stall. 'Holy cow' I thought as I stared at the tall figure in her sports skirt and trainers. How pretty she looked with her olive skin, shining hair and dark eyes, but best of all were her long, shapely legs. I swung into action at once, telling her all about life in England. Obviously impressed Katerine asked me if I would like to help her with her English homework? Would I? I could hardly get my answer out fast enough, but although I returned to my post each day, there was no further sign of her.

I began to lose hope until one day Franzeddy and I realized that the ticket buyer we were talking to was Katerine's aunt. I accepted her invitation to visit, and two days later Franzeddy pushed me to her house. There was Katerine, sitting in the front room. She suggested that we look at her photo album – usually a dreadful prospect – but on this occasion a good reason for sitting close to her. It was also a perfect excuse to pay her extravagant compliments whenever she appeared in a photograph. In need of privacy to enable me to further my cause, I asked to see the garden. Once outside, I discovered that Katerine did not have a boyfriend, so I turned on the charm even more. Katerine had just promised to give me a kiss when her father appeared. She agreed to walk some of the way home with me, and as we were strolling along Franzeddy, always the loyal friend, suddenly remembered she had to make an important phone call. She disappeared and I asked for my kiss. When it came, I thought: 'What on earth am I doing? Do I really want her after all?' Even now, six years later, I still don't know. I think I was subconsciously protecting myself from rejection or ridicule by extracting myself from a situation over which I had no control.

My hormones drove me on. Every female I met represented some kind of challenge, but it always ended in disappointment. I began to think that girls were openly flaunting themselves in front of me. They could bask in my obvious admiration without being threatened.

Mum was once more caught up in running the household, while I spent hours watching an endless procession of melodramatic and badly-written soap operas – the staple television diet in Colombia. The days were punctuated by the arrival of visitors, one of whom was Orlando, to his apparent disgust. Each day Eduardo forced him to follow the Colombian custom which requires a child of any age to ask for his mother's blessing in case one of them suddenly dies. I could not understand the change in my brother. He had always been such a friendly, helpful kid, with my best interests at heart. Now he was a sullen stranger who spoke only in monosyllables or cursed me if I spoke a word of English. He made me so angry that I longed to be able to hit him.

On reflection, I think Orlando's problem was that he was confused and his loyalties were torn. He had spent the first seven years of his life with his father, then he was sent off to England to begin a new and very different life, much of it centred around my needs. Now he was back in Colombia, he had his father to himself again, and was able to enjoy the admiration and affection shown by all his paternal relatives.

Sometimes Eduardo took me and my cousin Tania to the local swimming pool so I could watch the girls in their bikinis. We talked about the old days while Tania swum up and down the pool, and he hinted that it was Mum who had made the decision to leave him. He washed his hands of all blame. Why should she have minded his affairs with other women when he was providing such a good life for her? Although that made me feel hurt on Mum's

behalf, I still regarded Eduardo as my hero, and watched enviously
when he won dazzling smiles from the girls while my admiring
glances were received with disdain, as though I were a pervert.

On one of our trips to the swimming pool I sat, as usual, on the
front seat of the truck while Tania acted as my prop. By now she
was fourteen, beautiful, and out of bounds. After all, we had been
brought up together and she was practically my sister. Suddenly,
my floppy head fell forward on to her bosom. Unable to move, I
looked up to see Eduardo's knowing, salacious expression. My
cheeks were blazing as I asked Tania to sit me upright again. Little
did I realize then that my hero had designs on Tania himself.

21

Torn Between Two Worlds

After several happy months in Colombia, I began to hear worrying conversations about our return to England. The prospect was thoroughly depressing, despite the numerous farewell parties given in our honour. One of the most memorable took place in a nearby discotheque. It was rare to find one in a town centre because most of them are in out-of-the-way places, often near to motorways, so that married men can patronize them with ease and anonymity. Competition for the most beautiful girlfriend is rife in Colombia. If, however, the man's precautions fail and his wife finds out about his infidelity, he then abandons his girlfriend and prostrates himself before his wife, begging forgiveness. Promises of good behaviour and undying devotion are followed by extravagant presents. When Mum found about Eduardo's infidelity, she was given a new cooker, fridge and giant television. Some guilty, and presumably rich, husbands even go so far as to refurnish every room in the house in order to keep the peace. Many wives are happy to settle for such bribery, living as they do in a society which judges everyone by their possessions. Of course, once the dust has settled, the man carries on as before resorting to even more extravagant presents when he is discovered. However, Colombian men steer clear of affairs with married women, both through a sense of loyalty to their peers and as an act of self-preservation, because otherwise they risk revenge through reciprocal and shaming acts of adultery or even death. Needless to say, if a wife is unfaithful and found out, she is often thrown out of the home without further ado. Double standards are alive and well and living in Colombia.

That evening, I sat outside the night-club full of excitement at the prospect of furthering my education in the art of seduction. The doorman took one look at me and refused to let me in. 'He doesn't like people in wheelchairs. He thinks they are all mentally deficient' was my immediate thought, having once more forgotten that I was just fourteen years old! Mum came to the rescue by mentioning several influential friends, including Eduardo, and soon I was inside the natural hunting-ground of the Colombian male. I had managed to convince myself that being unable to dance didn't matter a bit. I had a secret weapon – my fascinating conversation. However, in spite of my outward bravado, I had to resort to Dutch courage.

Doctors had told me to steer clear of alcohol, but I pushed their warnings to the back of my mind as I joined the large party of family and friends. The combination of my small body and my inexperience with alcohol soon meant I was drunk and propositioning the first girl I saw. She was polite but definite – 'No.' That sobered me up enough to feel silly, but then I discovered a new and frightening sensation. I was losing control for the first time in my life. Panic took hold as I remembered my doctors' words: 'If you drink you could easily fall into an alcohol-induced sleep during which you may not be able to breathe properly. You could suffocate.' I was threatening my own life with my stupidity. To make matters worse, I looked up and saw my cousin Jairo dancing with the girl who had just turned me down.

As I sobered up, I tried to salvage my self-esteem by blaming the alcohol. I told myself that was the first and last time I would drink. As for the girls, I said to myself: 'There are plenty more fish in the sea. For all the ones who have refused me, there must be others who won't.'

We managed to delay our departure for another four weeks, but by then our money had run out and we had no choice. Although I hated the thought, I knew there was no future for me in Colombia – there was no health service and very little provision made for the disabled unless they happened to be extremely rich.

Mum, Orlando and I sat miserably at the airport, surrounded by a party of family and friends. Orlando sobbed loudly, clinging to his father like a baby monkey. As we struggled up the steps to the plane I saw the tears pouring down Mum's face as she dragged the hysterical boy behind her. I envied Mum for being able to show her emotions so openly. In my frantic search for something to concentrate on, I caught sight of my precious bag of souvenirs. During the flight, memories flooded back.

There was the old man in Palmira who stopped each day to talk as I sat at the window in the heat of the afternoon while the rest of the family slept. The day before we left he appeared with a parcel for me. I was thrilled to discover inside a catapult, beautifully carved in the shape of a naked woman.

Next I remembered the old man from Toro who had spent all his spare time digging for treasure. Country areas are full of legends about the Spanish conquests of the early sixteenth century. At first indigenous Indians welcomed the foreigners and gave them presents made from gold, which they believed to be the tears of the Sun God. But soon they learnt to fear the greedy invaders and buried their treasures in the jungle. To this day country people search for it. In over 40 years, my old man had found nothing but ancient pots and stone axe handles. I was now the proud owner of a collection of these.

Many hours later, half-dead with emotion and fatigue, we landed at Heathrow and approached the immigration desk. The officer took one look at us and began a series of pointed and hostile questions. Eventually he was persuaded that we had the right to be residents in Britain, but Orlando's cousin, who had travelled with us, was not so lucky and was marched off to a place of interrogation. We spent a nail-biting six hours waiting for him to reappear so that we could make our weary way home.

In spite of my reservations, I felt quite relieved to be back as I reflected on the difference in attitude between my two countries. It struck me that, in Colombia, the well-off and better educated either ignore the disabled or treat them almost as alien beings who are mentally retarded as well as physically handicapped. I remember the astonished looks people used to give me when they heard me speak with reasonable intelligence. The poorer Colombians, on the other hand, accept disability and do their utmost to help. In Britain, it seems to me, this state of affairs is often reversed. Whatever the case may be as far as attitude is concerned, practical help for the disabled is much more accessible in my adopted country.

Back in London, I felt the change keenly. In Colombia, I had come near to being a normal teenager and had had a taste of freedom. I could revel in the Latin American part of me, sit out in the open and make the most out of coming into contact with so many girls. Now life closed in on me once more, centred as it was around the living room instead of the doorstep. I felt less sure of my identity and brooded on how much I was dreading going back to school, where my outspoken approach worked against me.

It had been agreed that I would begin the GCSE course the following September. I looked forward to being able to sit public examinations in order to measure my abilities against those of my fellow pupils. However, I was disappointed when I heard that all my class had been entered at a fairly low level, removing any chance of gaining the top grades and also wiping out any true comparison with the results of my own age group in mainstream education. I understood that the teachers had neither the time nor the resources to cater for our separate needs, so they were forced to work at the pace of the weakest members of the class. My physical dependence on others left me with no choice in the matter, and, as my muscles continued to deteriorate my typing got slower than ever. It seemed that my head was always bursting with ideas which would never make it to the page.

Sadly, our English teacher became ill and was replaced by a succession of supply teachers for the rest of the year. Lessons grew increasingly disjointed as the whole class became experts in the art of testing and misleading each new member of staff.

By the end of the school year it was obvious that I was ill-prepared to pass my examination but, ever the optimist, I told myself: 'I can always make up for lost time when I get to college.' I returned to school in September, a month before my fifteenth birthday. We had a permanent English teacher at last but immediate difficulties arose when we discovered that all the course work we had produced the previous year, and which formed part of our examination work, was missing. We would have to go back to square one.

Our holiday in Colombia had reinforced our need to keep up the links. We began to save hard for our next trip and became ever more involved with the Latin American community in London. Orlando's cousin soon built up a network of contacts and included us in many activities. Mum had a Colombian boyfriend who took us to clubs and parties. He used to come and stay at weekends, when I would be moved into Orlando's bedroom where we sat up half the night watching videos. Everything went well at first, but after a while Orlando and I suspected that Mum's boyfriend was becoming increasingly distant. Perhaps he was jealous or felt we were in the way – particularly me. Even though I knew he was not a suitable candidate to be a stepfather, I was grateful to him for diverting Mum's attention away from my own attempts to have a love-life. She was forever trying to protect me from rejection and ridicule, but I had to fight my own battles on that front, even though the possibility of success was a long way off.

I would listen in disgust, perhaps tinged with envy, to the exaggerated boasts of my peers as they talked about their girlfriends. In Colombia, young men who discuss their sex lives are ostracised for ungentlemanly behaviour. My sense of frustration and powerlessness increased with each new disappointment. At least my weapon collection gave me a feeling of strength as I gazed at the fiercesome knives, whips and fire arms which I had saved up for or been given over the years.

My abortive attempts at finding a love-life lost their sting as soon as I thought about another visit to Colombia. It took nearly two years but as soon as we had saved enough, Mum booked our flights. We were to travel in November, the month after my sixteenth birthday. Four weeks before we were due to leave, I became ill with a chest infection. I felt under enormous pressure to get well in time. The day before we were due to leave I convinced myself that I was fit to travel.

Full of excitement, we set off in a friend's car which was piled high with luggage, oxygen cylinders, my wheelchair and medicines, happily ignorant of the twenty hours of horror that were to follow.

The trauma started in the car. I was looking out of the window while Mum and her friend chatted and suddenly realized that we were heading for the wrong airport. We wanted Gatwick, not Heathrow! When we finally arrived, the passengers for our flight were already boarding. Breathless and sweating, we rushed through the check-in desk and struggled up the steps of the plane. As Mum carried me down the aisle as fast as she could, one of my arms banged into the headrest of each seat we passed. I was convinced that it would end up broken. Orlando stumbled along behind us, lost under a mountain of luggage. We collapsed into our seats, only to realize that we were in a smoking area. My allergy to smoke intensifies when I have a chest infection. Sure enough, within minutes I could feel a burning sensation in my throat as it began to swell and ache.

From then on things went from bad to worse, beginning with our arrival in Paris where we were to wait for a connecting flight. Unable to get off the plane without help, we sat for forty minutes until two men appeared with what looked like a shopping trolley. They dropped me on to it and dragged it down the steps while I flopped about, head lolling backwards and legs stuck up in the freezing air. Once inside the airport building, I was laid out on a row of chairs whilst Mum went to find our luggage. As I lay there, unable to move, I tried to avoid meeting the eyes of onlookers, who clearly thought I was either lazy or drunk!

Once aboard the flight for Colombia, we realised our seats were again in a smoking area. Mum refused to sit down until we were moved. A grim night followed. My lungs had tightened up alarmingly and every other part of my body ached. The discomfort made me increasingly demanding. Every few minutes I asked Mum to move my head, arms or legs until she was exhausted. Unable to sit up now, I had to lie across Mum and Orlando. My brother was beside himself with worry as my breathing became more and more laboured. I even felt sorry for him, recognizing the enormous burden he had been forced to carry at such a young age.

The welcome cheer as we landed at last, in Bogatá, raised our spirits although, worryingly, I now felt as if I were being crushed by a massive weight, as I gasped for air.

'It must be tiredness,' I told myself firmly. 'I can't be ill. After all, I'm back in Colombia, and we're going to have another brilliant holiday. I've *got* to be all right.'

On the tarmac, the thin air of Bogotá made me increasingly breathless and light-headed, but I felt better when I saw Jairo, my faithful cousin, waiting for us in the airport terminal. He greeted us, and we set off to retrieve our luggage. We watched the carousel in mounting despair as it began to dawn on us that my cherished wheelchair was missing. What else was going to go wrong? That question was swiftly answered when we saw that Mum's suitcase had been slashed open. We were told that the wheelchair would be put on the next flight – in three days' time, but by now Mum was almost hysterical, knowing full well that any discomfort could make my life an utter misery which meant I always made sure everyone else suffered too.

I was shocked to find myself wishing that I were back in London, lying on my comfortable settee and watching television in peace, instead of being forced to face the indignity and worry associated with the journey. As I was manhandled up the steps of yet another plane I shouted in desperation: 'Why did you bring me to this rubbishy country where everyone is so bloody ignorant and they have no facilities for people like me?' Although I rarely mind creating a fuss when it comes to protecting my annoyingly vulnerable body, I soon felt deeply ashamed at this outburst against my beloved Colombia.

To keep my mind occupied with more positive thoughts, I returned to my all-consuming passion – sex! At sixteen I had officially reached manhood. The custom in country areas of Colombia, such as Toro, is for an older male – often an uncle – to take his young relative to a brothel, to be initiated into the delights of sex. My last few years in England had given me a more jaundiced view of that ritual, and it now seemed sleazy and embarrassing. 'All the same,' I told myself, 'beggars can't be choosers. If it has to be this way, so be it.'

At Cali airport I was put into yet another enormous rickety wheelchair. As I slithered about helplessly, feeling rather hard done by, I looked up to see a reception committee of nearly sixty people waiting for us in the arrivals lounge! I stared in astonishment at Tania and Gloria, who were even more lovely than I remembered them. Thank goodness I was wearing my new, expensive, fashionable clothes, including a pair of the latest trainers which provoked satisfyingly envious glances from my cousins.

Orlando departed joyfully with Eduardo and some of his relatives, and Mum and I went outside. There were about twenty cars, of all shapes and sizes, belonging to our party, but no one seemed in a hurry to leave. Gloria brought her boyfriend over to meet me, and as I took in her long legs and well-filled blouse, I realized that things would never be the same between us. She had grown up, whereas although I might be more intellectually advanced than Colombian boys of my age, I didn't have a clue when it came to relationships. I felt about ten years old.

Mum put me into the front seat of a truck and clambered in after me, wreathed in smiles. We sat there like sardines, dripping with sweat, while a big crowd of other people piled into the back of the truck. We set off, and unable to see out, I watched the driver with mounting anxiety. The Colombian standard of driving leaves a lot to be desired because it is based on frenzied, macho competition; even fourteen-year-olds are allowed to drive if they have passed the very minimal driving test. This driver seemed to be determined to break some sort of speed record, while jabbering over his shoulder to his passengers at the same time.

On that journey, whilst wondering if I were about to meet my Maker, I found myself becoming increasingly critical of Colombia and its lack of organization. Why weren't there more traffic lights, for a start, instead of it being every man for himself? It was as if I were seeing it all for the first time. Everything seemed so basic compared with Europe. Even so, this was still my country and I was already so immersed in the Spanish language that I wondered if I would ever think in English again.

22

Illness and Disillusionment

Somehow we survived the journey and arrived, still in one piece, at Aunt Esneda's home. Mum carried me into the familiar bedroom and laid me on the solid four-poster we shared. Twenty-five hours after leaving our London flat, I could at last lie down in peace. I looked around at the dark, heavy furniture, and realized for the first time how unsuitable it was for the small, cramped room and the suffocating heat. It was 40°C outside and not much less indoors. I thought I was going to melt.

Two days later, I knew that any hopes of an improvement in my health had been in vain. The old symptoms of burning at the back of my nose, painful throat and throbbing head returned with a vengeance. I lay in bed, feeling awful, and even the sight of my precious wheelchair, which had been collected by Eduardo and Orlando from Cali Airport, did nothing to raise my spirits. I couldn't face using it.

I had a long-standing invitation to go and stay with my aunt Consudo, Tania's mother, who was also my godmother, and although I protested that I was too ill, Mum said 'You'll just have to go – they might be offended if you don't – anyway it will do you good.'

It took ages to get me ready, especially as I was too weak to sit up unaided on Colin's commode. I wobbled from side to side under the shower; that was the last time I was able to use my commode for washing purposes. From then on I had to lie naked on the floor to be hosed down. Next, Mum gave me physiotherapy to try to clear my lungs. She lay me on the bed, draped over a special sponge wedge, with my head hanging down – in the 'postural draining' position. Then she banged my chest with cupped hands in order to trigger a cough so I could bring up some phlegm. She is expert at detecting exactly where the phlegm is thickest. Then she would shake and squeeze my chest to dislodge as much as possible.

Nando, my godmother's new, young husband came to collect me and took me to their home, but before long, it was obvious that I was getting worse, and eventually Mum had to be summoned. She arrived with Eduardo and Orlando, who had been paying her a duty visit. I was a little better in the cooler evening air, and still telling myself that I wasn't really ill, it was only a 24-hour bug. Mum returned home with the others, but by the following morning I could hardly breathe and she had to rush back and take me home. The next two days passed in a haze of feverish dreams, and when Eduardo came to visit he insisted that Mum should call a doctor. My supply of antibiotics hadn't made a scrap of difference to my illness and the phlegm in my lungs refused to shift. It was time to call for help.

Mum rang a doctor who had attended me as a child. After he had asked Mum several questions about how I was feeling she said: 'Please talk to Diego. He can tell you what is wrong much better than me.' I described my symptoms to him but, as he had never heard of muscular atrophy, he was nonplussed. He examined me and sounded my chest, then straightened up and announced that I was suffering from asthma. I retorted: 'I'm not an asthmatic. This is a muscular problem, not an allergic one.'

The doctor refused to change his opinion, and said I ought to be admitted to hospital. My blood ran cold, knowing that in Colombian hospitals the doctor's word is law and the patient is the last person to be considered. I said there was no way I would go into hospital while I was still conscious and Mum backed me up. We compromised by agreeing to hire a nurse to administer the drugs I needed intravenously. The drip would also feed me saline solution to prevent dehydration, which otherwise might easily kill me. Because of his conviction that I was asthmatic, the doctor also prescribed the drug Ventolin, which I had not heard of before.

The nurse arrived and the doctor explained her duties to her. He also decided that I needed oxygen, so Mum phoned numerous hospitals and private companies until at last she found a cylinder. It was very expensive and the company refused to deliver without advance payment. Mum had not changed enough money into local currency, and I was frightened of being without oxygen for too long, so Eduardo offered to pay.

Two days later, I realized that my body was reacting strangely to something. I shook uncontrollably, and even my tongue was affected so that I could barely speak. I knew about the effects of too much oxygen and of an allergy to antibiotics, but this was different. Everything pointed to the Ventolin.

I told Mum that I felt I was slowly dying, and that our old method of dealing with my chest infections was better than this. The nurse agreed that I was reacting badly to the Ventolin and removed it from the intravenous drip. When the doctor returned we thanked him for his attention and dispensed with his services. His bill was enormous. I realised then why Eduardo's father had gone bankrupt during his long illness.

Slowly, I began to improve. I was only able to sit up for an hour a day, so I lay in my room for most of the day and was visited by friends and relatives. Even so, I felt self-conscious about my appearance. I had lost so much weight that I was convinced I must look hideous.

Throughout this ghastly time, Eduardo was wonderful. He used to visit me two or three times a day, gave me a pocket television set and brought me fantastic take-away meals. For some reason I had gone off Mum's cooking.

Mum and I became quite good friends with a man who lived next door. Carlos was an economist and had a highly-paid job as well as running his own taxi company. I think he was keen on Mum, judging by his efforts to impress her. He would get one of his taxi-drivers to bring us food from a restaurant, and so on some nights I was given two meals, when it was as much as I could do to nibble at one.

Mum was running Ausnt Esneda's household again as was expected of her. Simon, Aunt Esneda's widowed husband, had gone to live with his new mistress so his children Jairo, Rodrigo and Gloria were left in Mum's care.

Gloria did not take kindly to Mum's concern about her – calling it interference. Things came to a head when Mum showed her disapproval of Gloria's boyfriend, who was playing truant from school to see her. Suddenly we were in the middle of a family feud and Gloria's father stopped helping with the household finances. Apparently he resented Mum playing mother to his daughter. In spite of the fact that Mum carried on looking after everyone, she and I were ostracised by the members of her family who lived in Palmira. Now we just had Carlos, Eduardo and Orlando for company.

One day, during the week before Christmas, without warning, my throat and lungs went into a sort of spasm. I had never experienced anything like it. Panic-stricken, I saw my life flash past. I thought: 'This is what it is like to drown.' I felt sure that I was going to die. Until now, I had often been on the verge of death but my survival had convinced me that God wanted to keep me alive for some special purpose. Now, fighting for breath, I wondered how important my mission on earth really was.

For weeks afterwards I had dreadful nightmares, full of claustrophobia and blindness. I could not wake up and, when I tried to, I saw thousands of people carrying huge words which I recognized from the calendar above my bed. Maybe it was my subconscious trying to deal with the prospect of death. Certainly, Mum's description of my behaviour during these nightmares bears this theory out. Apparently my eyes would open, I would go pale and then let out strangled screams. It was as though I were in another dimension, in a sort of straitjacket, desperately struggling to get back to life before I was pulled over to the other side.

One of my heroes, Simon Bolivar, said of his life, 'Death is an occupational hazard.' He might have been talking about me. Actually, death is a subject I avoid. Life is too enjoyable and too full of possibilities to waste time in thoughts of death. I think I am very lucky, and as far as I am concerned, the talents I possess make up for the deficiencies. I truly believe that almost anything is possible, even though I may have to work harder than most to achieve it. Mankind has a bargain with God. He gave us life, but the rest is up to us. All we need is determination and a belief in ourselves.

Christmas Eve arrived but I was still feeling ill and more and more disillusioned about the Colombian 'community spirit'. Mum decided that I really had to make an effort to get up, so she dressed me in my new Christmas outfit. Colombians take extra care with their clothes on special occasions, preferring to impress people with their sartorial elegance than with generous presents.

Mum was feeling as shattered, depressed and lonely as me, so I tried to put on a brave face. It was Christmas, after all. The trouble was I literally could not hold my head up, because I was too thin and weak. The effort of breathing while sitting up made me pour with sweat. Orlando visited us for half an hour, but made it clear that he would rather be at home with his father. I felt very resentful. My reliable and willing lieutenant had deserted me on the battlefield.

Aunt Miriam from Bienaventura was in Palmira to see her Grandmother. She popped in to see me, but her husband stayed in the car and refused to come into the house. It was another flying visit, and afterwards Mum and I looked at each other sorrowfully. I thought wistfully of Christmas in England. All I wanted at that moment was fog, snow and yet another repeat of *White Christmas* on the television. I felt so sorry for Mum, and more angry and betrayed on her behalf than on my own. Everyone in Colombia goes to a family party of some kind on Christmas Eve. But no-one seemed to want us. It seemed our feud with Simon and his family had affected our relationship with everyone else. If only Aunt Esneda were still alive. I know that she at least would not have become so impatient and bored with the prolonged illness which was the cause of our lonliness.

Christmas morning brought me my first album of salsa music – which I have loved ever since. Isolated from our family, Mum invited Carlos and a couple of other neighbours to join us for lunch – fish stew, vegetables and rice. Afterwards there was our traditional Colombian Christmas pudding – a sort of sweet toffee, always accompanied by a glass of milk. Then came the wine.

Christmas afternoon was enlivened by a visit from Nando who brought me several key-rings, because I had admired his set. That was the start of another collection, which is well over 100 strong now and comes from all over the world. The most interesting ones are what I choose to call 'artistic', although other people might prefer to call them plain rude!

Mum decided that we needed a New Year's Eve party. She invited the whole family in an effort to patch up our differences. Jairo opened our enormous bottle of duty-free whisky and guests started to arrive – Eduardo, my godmother, her husband, various uncles and cousins. The bottle of whisky was soon empty and before long two of the uncles were making uncharacteristically loud and derogatory comments about Eduardo and Carlos. The uncles taunted Eduardo for so long about his 'ostentatious' possessions, that he thought it would be sensible to hand his gun over to Mum for safe-keeping, and then leave with his shadow, Orlando. They soon returned in Eduardo's flashiest car, which he parked outside to irritate his tormentors further.

Things were hotting up. I sat back to watch the drama unfold. Out on the doorstep, I found my godmother, Consuelo, working herself into a frenzy over rumours concerning Eduardo and her daughter Tania, who was now sixteen. After a few more drinks, she announced that she was convinced Nando was being unfaithful. Tania became so embarrassed that she begged her mother to shut up, only to be rewarded with a slap in the face. She burst into loud sobs, shortly followed by her mother. Their noisy wails punctuated the rest of the evening.

Rodrigo added to the excitement by helping himself to the drinks provided by Mum and Eduardo and then taking them up the road to where Franzeddy was having her own party. When Jairo discovered what was going on, the brothers had a massive fight and had to be pulled apart in the middle of the street. As Eduardo got more and more drunk, it struck me that he preferred to be with Mum than his live-in girlfriend, who had been left at home. His eyes filled with alcohol-induced tears, as he embarked on a long, rambling bout of nostalgia about the good times we had once had together.

The noise reached a crescendo as everyone, except the quarrelsome uncles and the two sobbing women, became more and more silly and hysterical with laughter. Peace finally descended at about 9 o'clock the following morning, by which time several of the revellers had fallen asleep on the floor. I lay next to my rather tipsy mother. Every request I made for her to move me brought on a fit of the giggles. But I was happy that she was enjoying herself again.

A week later, Mum decided that I was well enough for her to be able to take a long weekend break. In order to make this possible Aunt Hilda arrived from Toroto to take over from Mum. Rodrigo agreed to do the necessary lifting, and my godmother promised to stay in every night to put me to bed, turn me during the night and get me up in the morning. Orlando was to provide the back-up for this plan. Mum also hired a maid to do the cleaning – not as extravagant as it sounds, as many of the Colombian poor happily do a day's work for a few pounds. It required a team of four to do what Mum does on her own. No wonder she needed a few days off from her duties.

I made little progress and we wondered if I would *ever* be well enough to make the journey back to England. The longer I stayed in Colombia's exhausting heat, the worse I became. We decided that it might help if we moved out of the city.

Consuelo and Tania had recently left their two small rooms and rented a large, cool, ventilated house on the outskirts of Palmira. We took up residence in the best room which was next door to the kitchen, so I was able to keep in touch with all the socializing that went on.

By this time, my godmother had no doubt that Nando had lost interest in her. She moped about listening to sentimental music, leaving Mum to run the household. The faithful Carlos still visited each evening, and took Mum to the market early on Saturday mornings. I rather approved of his courtship but the poor man never got a chance to be alone with Mum for long. I was always in the way.

Occasionally Mum and Carlos went out for a meal if Tania agreed to baby-sit. She often went to bed early at the other end of the house. I lay awake worrying about what would happen if my breathing went wrong or if someone broke in from the garden – I should be first in line for a bullet in the head! However, these anxieties were as nothing compared to my battle with the mosquitos which poured in from the tangled jungle outside. I lay listening to their maddening whines, furious that I could do nothing to prevent an attack.

Being so dependent on others, I spend much of my life sitting and observing. Perhaps this increases an awareness of my surroundings. One day, Mum, Tania and I were watching one of the numerous soap operas on television when I caught sight of Eduardo's shadow on the wall. He was standing round the corner

so that only Tania could see him. I watched the shadow beckon to
her, and she slipped out of the room. I told Mum what I had seen.
So, all the rumours had been true. We knew now why Tania would
get dressed up almost every evening and stay out until all hours,
refusing to say where she had been. My sixteen-year-old cousin had
lost her virginity to her own godfather. I was appalled – such a
relationship amounts to incest in Colombian culture. Another feud
developed. This time between Mum and my godmother who was
not prepared to do anything about the scandalous situation. Things
got so bad that Mum and I avoided being in the house. It felt just
as it had done seven years earlier when we were driven out of
Grandmother's flat in London. I must admit, though, that part
of me enjoyed the situation. Mum and I were together, fighting a
common enemy and I was the chief strategist, devising plans to
outwit our foes.

At least the loyal Carlos never let us down. On my good days he
would take me for a drive through the parts of town which most
fascinated me. I loved to look at the huge, flamboyant mansions
owned by the very rich. Peering through enormous wrought-iron
gates, I watched armed guards patrolling with vicious dogs and
imagined one day owning the treasures they were protecting. At
the other end of the city lay the red light district. Driving through
its gaudy streets was particularly thrilling. As I wondered what lay
behind the frilly curtains, I fantasised about being able to visit the
area in my own limousine. Carlos and I gave each girl a grading, in
between bouts of laughter and crude remarks.

Several pimps offered to take me to a brothel but, sadly, I had to
turn their offers down. I knew that my fragile health would not
stand up to the excitement. If only I had been well, I would have
agreed like a shot. After all, my total lack of mobility need not be a
problem – I was sure the lady in question would be able to deal
with that!

It was Carlos who again came to our rescue when Mum and I
decided to visit Toro and stay with Aunt Hilda for the weekend.
We planned to have an early night, in readiness for a 5 o'clock start
the following morning, but my godmother decided to throw a
massive party that evening in an effort to cheer herself up. Mum
and I lay in bed, vainly trying to get some sleep, while the music

got louder and louder. In desperation we decided to get dressed and leave for Toro at once, although, with me, nothing can ever happen 'at once'. As part of the 'getting ready' ritual, Mum pushed me, half-naked, to the toilet. To my horror, we came face to face with a stunning girl, who stared openly at me, first with surprise and then with pity. All she could see was a small, misshapen figure being pushed like a baby. There was no chance to impress her with my 'intelligence and erudition'! Ready at last, we were waiting for Carlos' driver to arrive when a huge commotion suddenly broke out. My godmother shrieked at Nando about his infidelity, and then tried to stab him with a kitchen knife. Jairo attempted to restrain her, but she rushed into her bedroom, sobbing uncontrollably. Then she came in to me and begged my forgiveness for her recent behaviour and for the feud which had developed between us. I felt a kind of power in the situation but took no delight in it. I could hardly bear to watch her humiliation as she bent down towards me, her face streaked with tears and make-up. I remembered her fierce defence of me when strangers made unkind comments. Now I was the one trying to reassure her.

At last we were on our way, accompanied by Orlando at Mum's insistence. We arrived in the early morning to be greeted emotionally by Aunt Hilda. It was wonderful to be made so welcome. I was carried in and laid down on a bed. This was turning out to be a holiday which consisted of going from one bed to another. Aunt Hilda brought us a local speciality called *guiso*, which is a soup made from couscous. I felt quite content.

Later that day, Orlando and I heard the sound of an engine, obviously belonging to a big car. It was Eduardo's. Orlando shot out to meet his father and insisted on going home with him. I was furious and hurt. Could he really not bear to stay with Mum and me? I was also angry with Eduardo and felt I could no longer communicate with him. I could never forgive his unnatural liaison with Tania, or his failure to live up to my image of him as a hero.

Having recently tried to analyze my rather ambivalent feelings for Eduardo, I have reached the conclusion that, at sixteen, I almost blamed him for not being the father I longed for so much. Yet, I would tell myself sternly: 'Well, he *isn't* your dad, so you'd better get used to it.' I know now that no one could have lived up to the idealized image I had of him, but at the time the knowledge that he had feet of clay made me feel bereft and betrayed. I also suffer from a sense of guilt at my rejection of the man who always showed me affection and generosity. Eduardo was killed in a car crash when I was nineteen, two and-a-half years after his affair with Tania. I had refused to speak to him for all that time. Orlando lost his beloved father and I lost a good friend.

23

A Pilgrimage and Reluctant Farewells

On our first Sunday in Toro, we set off for Aunt Chela's old home. It felt like a pilgrimage, returning to the scene of so many happy memories, the home where I was king and loved unconditionally by all the members of Mum's close-knit family. We approached the house full of expectation but when we arrived it looked neglected and lonely. My heart sank as we went in through the front door. Half the brick flooring of the passage lay in piles of rubble, and doors hung off their hinges. Worse was to come. Aunt Chela's precious garden, which had produced so much of our food, was now home to a colony of weeds. Most shocking of all, there was a man in the garden committing the worst possible sin of all – picking what remained of the fruit in the full heat of the midday sun. Aunt Chela and her sisters would never have done such a thing. They were convinced that picking fruit during the heat of the day would result in permanent damage to the tree.

I saw Aunt Chela's house and garden as a symbol. It had once represented the closeness of our extended family, with its clearly defined hierarchy. With so many of my beloved elders gone, I would never again enjoy the certainty, stability and security they had given me. Another piece of my childhood had been destroyed.

Mum, like all ex-patriot Colombians, always dreamed of owning a tiny piece of her own country. Her savings, considerably boosted by Eduardo's 'presents' enabled her now to put down the deposit on a small bungalow which needed renovation. Once it was habitable we were able to move in. Mum had already found some tenants, and they were persuaded to let us use one of the rooms in return for a reduced rent and shared housework. I almost lived in our room, so as to keep out of the way of the builders who were still working on the rest of the house. Although my health appeared to improve whenever the weather got cooler, I still couldn't sit up for more than an hour at a time.

Mum's bungalow is typical of the small properties in Colombian towns. Each one faces on to the street and proclaims its individuality by means of tiled and railed colonisation of the wide pavement. The ornate metal front door is divided into three sections. Usually, only one section is used as a doorway but, during heavy rain, the whole thing is pulled back so the house can double as an emergency garage. Colombians love their cars so much that they will happily share their homes with them when necessary. There is invariably one huge window at the front of the house, through which passers-by can glimpse the living room – the contents advertise the family's place in society. The size of the window increases in direct proportion to the owners' pride in their possessions. The bedrooms lie at the back of the house, and look on to the walled garden. A traditional washing platform, fitted out with a cold-water tank and a tap, is built into one of the patio walls. Only the wealthy can afford washing machines, and even then they are often unused – Colombian women generally prefer to scrub the clothes by hand, so they can actually watch the dirt coming out! Our own dirty clothes took on a new significance when it came to washing me. Colin's dual purpose commode was no longer with us, so Mum covered the tiled floor of the shower-room with unwashed linen and placed me, like a naked baby, on top. She quickly learnt to keep certain parts of my anatomy out of range of the powerful jets of water!

After several weeks in our little house, Mum and I decided that my health had improved and I was sufficiently robust for us to risk the flight back to England. Before we left though, Mum took me on a pilgrimage to El Señor de Los Milagros – a giant crucifix in the sixteenth-century cathedral in Buga, a city to the north of Palmira.

Jairo and Orlando hauled me up the steep, narrow flight of steps which led to a small, flower-filled chapel in which about fifty pilgrims were praying for a miracle. The focus of attention was a life-sized figure of Christ on the cross, protected by a glass barrier. I felt a great sense of relief at being so close to God. He would surely protect me if I deserved it. As usual, I prayed in my own way rather than reciting the standard Catholic prayers.

We left the small chapel and attended Mass in the main cathedral, leaving by the back entrance. Once outside I was horrified to see several miserable, tattered beggars propped up against a wall. As I looked at their ulcerated legs and pinched faces I was hit by the hypocrisy of our society. We and the rest of the congregation were leaving the cathedral, feeling cleansed and confident, having asked for miracles and confessed our sins. Then we passed by these poor creatures who would have been delighted with a little food and some clean clothes, or even a few coins. I realized how lucky I am to have a family who love and care for me, and I wondered how some members of my faith can allow so much wealth to be on display to the glory of God while ignoring the plight of these people, who belong to God just as much as the church-goers.

Having placed ourselves in the hands of the Almighty, we paid for our seats home with the last of our cash. Mum had to cancel the bookings twice when my health deteriorated yet again. Understandably, the airline officials were by now reluctant to have me on board. They demanded a medical certificate which Eduardo obtained from a doctor friend who owed him a favour. The doctor did not set eyes on me! Mum came to the conclusion that my health kept failing because of a subconscious fear of the long ordeal ahead of me. I think she was probably right. Anyway, we managed to leave on the third booking.

Carlos drove us to Cali, where we waited for the internal flight to Bogotá. A true friend, Carlos had insisted he fly to Bogotá with us and see us safely on our way to Britain. As we sat in the crowded waiting room, I felt torn between my longing to remain in Colombia and my need for the security of life in Britain. It was as if I were leaving my family behind to go and stay with a good friend – a friend to whom I owed my life, but who could never alter my passionately Colombian identity. My anguish increased as I realized that I might even be risking my life by flying. On the other hand, if I did not leave Colombia soon, I would be risking it anyway.

We boarded what looked like an elderly and unkempt reject from an American airline. In a thoroughly nervous state, I began to wonder if we would even make it off the ground. Once in the air,

however, things looked better, but as we began our descent to
Bogotá the air pressure seemed to change and I began to suffocate.
Panic-stricken and drenched with sweat, I gasped: 'Mum, I
can't breathe. Lie me down.' She leaped to her feet and asked the
stewardess to bring my oxygen. Twenty long seconds passed
before the mask was placed over my face. As I lay in a limp heap, I
realized that I had wet myself. I saw pity mixed with fascination in
the faces of the other passengers, and helpless terror in those of
Carlos and Orlando. It was bad enough for Orlando to be leaving
his father without having to see his elder brother apparently dying
in front of him. He must have been totally unnerved.

When we landed in Bogotá, its rarefied air did nothing to help
matters. Mum wheeled me to the airport hospital, by which time
I was sweating so profusely that I was convinced I was now suffering from malaria!.

Worse was to come. Mum and Carlos discovered that the travel
agent had not confirmed our seats to London. Mum pleaded
with the airline official, but she was adamant that no seats were
available. 'My son will die if we don't get away from the thin air of
Bogotá today!' Mum yelled, but it made no difference until Carlos
insisted on seeing the manager. As soon as he arrived, Carlos
handed over his business card, proving that he was a high-ranking
official in a large and powerful electricity company. Suddenly, all
was sweetness and light. Seats on the flight miraculously became
available and a supply of oxygen was arranged for me.

It was a four-hour wait for our flight; just enough time for me to
work myself up into a state of terror at the thought of what lay
ahead. 'I just can't do it,' I gasped. 'I'm sure I will die.' Carlos had to
break the news to the manager, who luckily showed no sign of
resentment at having to cancel our hard-won seats.

Once again Carlos came to the rescue by arranging for us to stay
with a friend. The house was elegant and spotless. Mum laid
me down on the tiled floor for fear of using the grand, silk-covered
settee. The mistress of the house gazed at me disapprovingly and
then dispatched the four of us to a simple room. During the following three nights I must have driven Mum and Carlos mad with lack
of sleep as, in my desperation to breathe comfortably, I asked to be
moved over and over again. During the daytime, Orlando and I

stayed in our room while Mum and Carlos tried to rearrange our flights.

We moved yet again. This time to an acquaintance named Maria who lived in a tiny, humble house. Our reception could not have been warmer. Back in the thin air of Bogotá my need for oxygen became all too apparent. I worried about becoming an addict, but after four days without it, I was forced to acknowledge my dependence. Carlos phoned a private supplier and I was attached to a lifeline. It was like being reborn. At last we could all sleep through the night. The cost was prohibitive, however, so I did without oxygen during the day, except during mealtimes so I could eat properly.

My inability to get to a bathroom or to sit upright made toileting extra-complicated. Mum was forced to place a bucket near the edge of the bed, and I lay above it with my bottom in mid-air and my feet dangling towards the floor. The whole performance was so difficult and uncomfortable that it seemed to go on for hours, but there was no alternative. I suppose most people would feel embarrassed, but to me it was just another interesting experience caused by my disability. It is not everyone who flies half-way round the world to have a shit in a bucket!

On the Saturday, Mum and Carlos visited a shrine, where Mum prayed yet again for me to be well enough to travel to London, promising God that if he helped, she would one day return as a pilgrim. Carlos had been away from his office for too long. Tearfully, he left us on the Monday night. Ten days dragged by as we lived in limbo until the day of our flight.

At the airport, Maria's son, José took off his *escapulario* and handed it to me, saying: 'Have faith and God will look after you.' To this day, I wear the two small leather-bound pictures of Christ and the Virgin Mary.

Once more we managed to cause an upheaval. Our friend, the airline manager, decided we should board the plane before everyone else. Crowds of passengers were held back as I was wheeled past them feeling so weak and ill that I could not even thank the manager for his help. He looked at me pityingly, apparently convinced that I would never make it, which was a view shared by the captain and the chief steward who met us in the cabin. They demanded a copy of the doctor's letter which stated I was fit to make the journey, and insisted that Mum sign a document relieving them of all responsibility in the event of my death. Not very reassuring. Mum turned to me and said: 'Well, Diego, it's all up to you.'

Once we had taken off, I could breathe more easily, and even sat upright in my seat. By the time we were on the last leg of the journey, however, from Paris to Gatwick, exhaustion took over. I begged the stewardess to let me lie down, but none of the passengers would move from their seats. For once I felt violent anger at the insensitivity shown by some of the able-bodied.

Gatwick at last! I felt quite euphoric. My wheelchair appeared as if by magic and a member of the airport staff arrived to push me, while Mum and Orlando struggled with our bags. When he heard us speaking Spanish, the man turned to a colleague and said: 'Trying to get into the country illegally. Probably smuggling drugs, as well.' After a while, I said, in my best English: 'Excuse me, have you worked here long? Perhaps you would be good enough to tell me which team won the FA Cup?' His face was a picture.

Grandmother, once so hostile, was waiting for us, her face wreathed in smiles. We had been away for five months and it had taken us eighteen days to get from Palmira to London. As I lay on the back seat of the taxi, my excitement grew. I was going home – to my own bed, my television and stereo and, above all, to my reliable and friendly GP.

As it turned out, they weren't all I was going back to. As soon as we had finished telling my doctor about the state of my health in Colombia, and he had listened to my chest, he sent me straight to King's College Hospital.

24

In Pursuit of Excellence

I have been in hospital more times than I care to remember but, although this visit turned out to be the most serious for several years, it also proved to be the most fortunate. As I lay in my cubicle in the children's ward, an oxygen mask covering my face, I had little to do but to take stock of my life. The future looked, at best, somewhat uncertain. For various reasons, my education have proved to be piecemeal and unsatisfactory. The new academic year was approaching, but, even if I had been eager to return to school, I could not yet sit up for long enough to cope with even half a day in class. At sixteen, I had missed out on the only opportunity to prove myself in the one way open to me – through academic achievement. I had not even one G.C.S.E. to my name.

I had made some enquiries about the possibility of Home Tuition but was told very firmly that I was not entitled to it. I must either attend school or college, which was not an option in my state of health. It looked as though there was nothing to look forward to except lying in front of the television all day. However, my natural optimism asserted itself and I thought, 'Something will turn up. It usually does.'

It did. In the form of the Teacher-in-Charge of the Hospital Tuition Unit. When I saw Jill Rutherford peering tentatively into my cubicle before coming in, I thought 'Yet another doctor about to prescribe yet another treatment. Still she's the best-looking one I've seen so far!' Before long we were deep in conversation in spite of my rather gasping and inaudible contribution. Jill listened patiently while I talked about my life, its frustrations and my desperate need to do something worthwhile. Her obvious interest in what I had to say began to restore some of the belief I had in myself. Surely I should find a way to show the world that, despite being severely disabled physically, I was more than competent mentally.

During one of our daily 'lessons' Jill remarked 'Your life has been so interesting you should write the story down.' 'I'd love to' I replied 'but of course, I can't'. Jill suggested that we might do it together and I agreed with alacrity, although privately thinking 'She means well but probably nothing will come of it'. I was wrong.

At last my chest infection cleared but I was still weak and floppy when I returned home at the end of July. A series of postcards arrived from the Far East where Jill was visiting two of her children. On her return she began the regular visits which were to last for over four years during which she listened to my sometimes muddled and rambling reminiscence, hauling me back as I wandered off down some autobiographical byway.

At first, although Jill was always extremely easy to talk to, I wondered if I should be able to speak honestly about everything and especially about the more intimate details of being disabled. I need not have worried. No-one could have been more unshakeable, understanding or unpatronising. Before long Jill and I were enjoying many a heated discussion on a wide range of subjects from religion and literature to sex and food. Inevitably we considered what appeared to be my rather bleak future. Annoyed by the negative response I had received from my Local Education Authority, Jill took up cudgels on my behalf. Before long she gave me the thrilling news that I was to study for GCSE English. Somehow she had managed to persuade the Headteacher of the local individual Tuition Centre to allow one of her staff to teach me for several hours each week. I felt as though I had won the Lottery. At last I was on my way.

I looked forward eagerly to meeting my tutor. Would she regard me as arrogant and argumentative as had so many of my teachers? When Dr Edite Mason, a tiny fragile-looking woman, walked into my room, my first thought was 'Oh dear, she'll be no match for my egocentricity and outspoken approach'. Yet again I was proved wrong. Edite's outward appearance belied a strong, forceful personality combined with a gentle, understanding nature. For someone who had taught a range of students from graduates to pupils who had been excluded from their schools, I hardly posed a problem! Within a very short time I began to appreciate my luck in acquiring such an inspired teacher. I realised too, how little I really knew my adopted language and its literature. However Edite, like Jill, gave me confidence in my ability and at the same time succeeded in curtailing my verbosity and flights of fancy. I looked forward to each lesson, revelling in the acquisition of real knowledge and the sense of achievement that it brought.

Half-way through the year Edite had to go into hospital for a serious operation. I am ashamed to admit that I felt quite as sorry for myself as I did for her. During the next six weeks I went back to my only other teacher, the television set. I also tried to read – a laborious process which entails my lying on one side and prodding at the pages with a rubber-tipped stick held in my three 'working' fingers.

Once Edite was back we had to make up for lost time. It was easy for me – I just listened and talked whilst she had to write down my thoughts, help me to assemble them more effectively and type up the results. August arrived and I received my first mark for a public examination, a starred A. After years of blowing my own trumpet, I finally had concrete proof that my disabled body housed a capable mind. But the euphoria did not last long. One GCSE in English Literature was hardly enough to set me on course for a brilliant career. Jill and Edite managed to ensure that, in spite of the Local Education Authority's continued insistence that I was not entitled to home tuition, the more enlightened headteacher of the tuition centre gave her support. She agreed to allow Edite to tutor me for A Level English. I also wanted to take GCSE Spanish but for this I would have to find a private tutor. Once again Jill and Edite swung into action, bombarding various educational charities until we had the necessary funding.

My Spanish tutor, Jane, became another friend. Quiet and concerned, she brought out a side of myself which I found quite surprising. Her gentleness prevented me from inflicting on her the more contentious and egocentric side of my nature. However, her diffidence lessened when she began to understand how little I need to be handled with kid gloves. Jill recognised very early on in our relationship that I thrive on 'debate', whereas my weekly conversations with Colin are different again. His refusal to be drawn into verbal combat can be thoroughly frustrating. Ever the pragmatist and peacemaker, he neatly side-steps my attempts to draw him into an argument. However, over the years, I have grown to respect and value Colin's integrity and his opinions on a wide range of subjects. Nick, the longest-serving member of what Jill calls my 'entourage', is also difficult to provoke because I have come to share many of his ideas. It is to him that I usually turn first for answers to questions concerning anything from religion and philosophy to money and power.

Another August and two more results. Both top grades. There was sufficient money left in the kitty to enable me to ask Jane to tutor me for A Level Spanish but I should still not be qualified to go on to further education and I was nearly nineteen. With just ten days to go before the start of the new academic year, Jill and I discussed the situation. 'Why shouldn't you go to college now?' she asked. With that, she was on her way to the local college for further education demanding to talk to various tutors and, more importantly, to the co-ordinator for students with Special Educational Needs. By the end of the week her persistence had paid off. I was offered a place to study A Level Government and Politics. The Local Education Authority had agreed to make this possible by providing transport to and from the college, an attendant to push me around and act as my amanuensis and someone else to transcribe my taped essays.

The course was to last two years so there would be plenty of time to study another subject. After so many hours spent discussing philosophy with Nick he agreed to formalise our Friday evening sessions by coaching me for the AS Level Philosophy examination. I was delighted.

As the beginning of term approached, I felt both excited and apprehensive. I had not been in formal education for nearly four years and never in a mainstream setting. Recent lessons had been tailored to my specific needs by committed teachers in the safety of my own home. I wondered whether my attendants would be able to cope if I became ill, but at that moment nothing could detract from my eagerness to make the most of the opportunity to prove myself once more by challenging the tutors and outshining my fellow pupils.

On the first day of the course a taxi delivered me to the steps of the college where an attendant was waiting to wheel me into the classroom. I watched with interest as the students quickly divided into two quite separate groups – one black and one white. As I Colombian, I wondered which one I should fit into. I soon found out. Neither. For over a year, during the two days on which I attended college each week, no-one but the tutor spoke to me. My attendant and I formed our own group of two.

Sometimes I felt that I should be the first to make an approach but was always prevented from doing so by a sense of awkwardness. My appearance and the presence of a wheelchair somehow created a barrier to normal relationships with my peers.

I resolved that, although I may be a misfit socially, nothing was going to hold me back academically. I would prove that I was better than all the others put together. The tutors responded to my enthusiasm and determination to answer their every question before anyone else had a chance. My essays, spoken into a tape recorder and laboriously transcribed, gained the highest marks. I revelled in my studies ignoring the fact that my academic success and apparent lack of modesty could hardly have endeared me to my fellow students. They continued to avoid contact with me although one or two managed to say 'Hello' as they passed by in the corridor.

One day my attendant decided that she was tired of sitting alone in the classroom with me during the morning break. She disappeared to find a coffee. As the tutor also prepared to go, he noticed my discomfort, even panic, at the prospect of being left completely on my own. He wheeled me down to the canteen and placed my wheelchair next to some of my classmates, saying 'Look after Diego' to one young man. Within seconds the rest of the group had melted away leaving their unfortunate friend sitting next to me in a state of acute embarrassment. I did my best to help him to relax by making cheerful conversation. Without success. The poor chap muttered monosyllabic answers as he looked anywhere but at me. I'm not sure who was the more relieved when he was able to leave me in my accustomed position in the classroom and return to the safety of his group.

My 'separateness' was further confirmed on a visit, during the second year of our course, to a careers exhibition in North London. As my attendant wheeled me past the various stands we crossed paths with several of the six remaining students in our class. Each one of them studiously ignored me. Fascinated by their reaction, I tried to make sense of the situation. Perhaps they were just shy but it was also evident that one or two of the boys resented me for being different. Somehow their maleness was threatened and they were compelled to despise me for not being what they considered to be a 'proper' man. The girls were more soft-hearted but they too appeared to feel that their image would be spoiled if they were caught talking to me.

Anyway, I was more interested in discovering what was on offer. I found out all I could about degree courses and career possibilities, returning home full of grandiose plans for the future. I would read Law in London so that I could live at home. The undergraduate day was sure to be exhausting for someone as severely disabled as I, but at least I should be able to return each evening to my own home in the knowledge that Mum and Orlando would be there as usual to look after me. About two months later I found myself waiting eagerly for the post each day.

Three letters arrived. To my horror, a refusal from my first choice, the London School of Economics. The others offered me interviews which I attended at once. I was astonished at the difference between the two. The Head of the Faculty of Law at University College, after asking me relevant academic and personal questions, described the college facilities for the disabled with particular reference to my extremely dependent situation. He asked whether my Local Education Authority would provide a grant, transport and full-time attendant. I replied blithely,' Oh yes, that will be all right' whilst thinking to myself 'I'll fight that battle when I come to it'.

A week later I was driven to my second interview. The Law tutor gazed at me doubtfully as I was wheeled in. His pessimistic attitude increased throughout the next forty-five minutes, only five of which were spent talking about my chosen subject. For the rest of the time my inquisitor asked probing questions relating to my health, or lack of it, and to my medical prognosis. His train of thought was transparent, 'What is the point of us giving a place to this incredibly disabled chap when he might go and die on us in the middle of, or soon after, he has finished his degree course. That is, if he is capable of doing it at all.' When he went on to discuss the almost complete lack of facilities for the disabled at the college, I knew that there would be no place there for me.

When I next spoke to Edite she advised me to appeal to the London School of Economics to reconsider my application. I dictated what I thought was a quite irresistible letter, enclosing testimonials from my tutors and a note from my doctor. I also telephoned the Student Welfare and Disability Officer at the LSE who offered me his support.

Ten days later, a letter arrived asking me to attend an interview with two professors, one of whom had special responsibility for co-ordinating arrangements for disabled students. The two men grilled me for almost an hour, taking it in turns to ask penetrating questions. It was evident that their main concern was my aptitude for a demanding academic course rather than with the problems presented by my physical handicap. My own worries on that front were soon alleviated when the Student who was the Union representative for the disabled took me on a tour of the buildings which were very well-adapted for the wheelchair user. I felt even better when I discovered that the University had its own medical staff and health centre where students could rest during the day if necessary.

On the journey home in a taxi, accompanied by my attendant from college, I hardly dared to hope that I might actually be given the chance to join the ranks of the famous and eminent people who had begun their careers at the LSE. I had been offered a place at University College provided that my examination results were high, but somehow that was not enough. The LSE was my first choice.

It was to be six weeks before the letter arrived. I did my best to appear calm as Orlando opened it and said 'Diego, you'd better read this.' It was an unconditional offer of a place at the London School of Economics to read for a degree in Law!

Five years ago I felt as though I were stuck at the bottom of a hill with no apparent means of climbing up it. My education so far had been a failure and I knew that someone in my condition could succeed on an equal footing only though academic achievement. However, in spite of a sense of frustration I cannot remember ever losing hope. I believed that God would provide enough footholds to enable me to begin my ascent. Besides I have always been convinced that I have a kind of destiny to fulfill. Now, at 21, I find myself half-way up the hill. I am well aware that the path to the top may prove dangerous and arduous and that I could be pushed off it at any time. But I thrive on challenge.

Because of my enforced imobility, I spend a great deal of time in thought More often than not I find myself looking into the future.

I see a crowded, oak panelled courtroom. The focus of attention is a figure addressing a spellbound audience. He is wearing a wig and a black silk gown. He is seated in a wheelchair.

The Jennifer Trust for Spinal Muscular Atrophy

Registered charity Number 327669

The work of The Jennifer Trust for Spinal Muscular Atrophy (JTSMA)

The JTSMA was founded in April 1985 following the death of Jennifer Macaulay from Werdnig-Hoffman Syndrome at the age of seven months. It is a national support group run by parents and adults affected by the physical disability, Spinal Muscular Atrophy. The main aim of the group is to provide information, understanding and friendship to those in need.

SMA What it is

Spinal muscular atrophy (SMA) is a genetically inherited condition of the anterior horn nerve cells in the spinal cord. SMA results in the wasting and weakening of muscles. Weakness can be severe and progressive, but varies according to SMA type. SMA also affects the respiratory system, causing difficulties in breathing and coughing.

The genes which cause the childhood types of SMA are 'recessive' and inherited from our parents. Recessive genes are those which we inherit but which do not show as characteristics in ourselves. If a couple both have the SMA recessive gene, then the chance of their offspring being affected is 1 in 4. One in 50 people in the UK carry the SMA gene.

SMA The types

Type I
Werdnig-Hoffmann condition, Acute infantile SMA or severe SMA

This is the most severe form of SMA. Its effects are always seen within the first six months of a child's life. Within a few weeks or months after birth, weak muscles cause the babies to have difficulty rolling over, lifting their heads or sitting unsupported. Difficulties in breathing and consequent respiratory conditions often make it unlikely that such children will live to their second birthday.

Type II
Intermediate SMA or Chronic infantile SMA

This form of SMA resembles Type I in that it starts in infancy (usually between 6–12 months). However it does not have the rapid and relentless progression of Type I. Most children are unable to sit unsupported and very few learn to crawl or walk. Clinical progression of the condition is slow, with most reaching adult life and becoming highly intelligent people.

Type III
Kugelberg-Welander condition, Chronic proximal SMA or mild SMA

This is a mild form of SMA, usually noticed after the child has learned to walk, and usually after the age of two. Most children can sit up, crawl, and walk, though the actions are slow. Progression of the condition is very slow but most having a long and active life.

Adult onset

There are thought to be several types of Adult Onset SMA, which do not link to the childhood SMA gene. Muscles weaken during life, though progression varies and often allows a full and active life. Research has not proved that Adult Onset is inherited.

* * *

To find out more about spinal muscular atrophy contact The Jennifer Trust for Spinal Muscular Atrophy. JTSMA has area contact families who provide local support and advice and are experienced in SMA.

A quarterly newsletter *Holding Hands* is produced and an annual conference weekend is held offering the opportunity to meet professionals, and others in similar situations in both formal and informal surroundings.

National Head Office:
Jennifer Trust for Spinal Muscular Atrophy
11 Ash tree Close
Wellesbourne
Warwickshire
CV35 9SA

Tel: 01789 842377
Fax: 01789 268371
e-mail: anita@jtsma.demon.co.uk.

Executive director: Anita Macaulay
Chairman: Craig Hamilton
Patrons: Professor V Dubowitz, BSc, MD, PhD, FRCP, DCH
                     Jane Horrocks

Your local Contact Family:
Contact Head Office to find out who your local Contact Family is.

All publishers proceeds from sales of *Diego's Story* will go to the Jennifer Trust for Spinal Muscular Atrophy